MENTORING
TEACHERS

The New Teacher Center

New Teacher Center focuses on improving student learning by accelerating the effectiveness of new teachers. NTC partners with states, school districts, and policy makers to implement programs that create sustainable, high-quality mentoring and professional development; build leadership capacity; work to enhance teaching conditions; improve retention, and transform schools into vibrant learning communities where all students succeed.

MENTORING TEACHERS

Navigating the Real-World Tensions

Ann Lieberman, Susan Hanson,
Janet Gless

FOREWORD BY ELLEN MOIR

Sponsored by New Teacher Center

JOSSEY-BASS
A Wiley Imprint
www.josseybass.com

Published by Jossey-Bass
A Wiley Imprint
One Montgomery Street, Suite 1200, San Francisco, CA 94104-4594
www.josseybass.com

Jossey-Bass books and products are available through most bookstores. To contact Jossey-Bass directly call our Customer Care Department within the U.S. at 800-956-7739, outside the U.S. at 317-572-3986, or fax 317-572-4002.

Wiley also publishes its books in a variety of electronic formats and by print-on-demand. Some material included with standard print versions of this book may not be included in e-books or in print-on-demand. If the version of this book that you purchased references media such as CD or DVD that was not included in your purchase, you may download this material at http://booksupport.wiley.com. For more information about Wiley products, visit www.wiley.com.

Library of Congress Cataloging-in-Publication Data
Lieberman, Ann.
    Mentoring teachers : navigating the real-world tensions / Ann Lieberman, Susan Hanson, Janet Gless ; Foreword by Ellen Moir ; Sponsored by the New Teacher Center.
        p. cm.
    Includes index.
    ISBN 978-0-470-87412-7 (pbk.); ISBN 978-1-118-13893-9 (ebk.);
    ISBN 978-1-118-13894-6 (ebk.); ISBN 978-1-118-13895-3 (ebk.)
    1.   Mentoring in education—United States. 2.   Teachers—United States.
3.   Interpersonal relations—United States.   I. Hanson, Susan, date. II. Gless, Janet. III. Title.
    LB1731.4.L54 2012
    371.1020973—dc23

                                                                    2011032503

Printed in the United States of America
FIRST EDITION
PB Printing 10 9 8 7 6 5

CONTENTS

v

CONTENTS

PART TWO · STORIES OF MENTORING

FOREWORD

When I was working in the schools in Santa Cruz, California, I saw many teachers in their first year — often the most talented teachers — want to quit. They felt unsuccessful and were concerned that they weren't able to prepare all of their students for academic success. Around that time, a group of us had an opportunity to help new teachers develop a solid base for their teaching. We realized that the first two years, called the "induction" years, are crucial in a teacher's career. So we began to build what we called "instructional mentoring" during those induction years. The big idea was to mentor beginning teachers in such a way that they would help all of their students learn, regardless of their socioeconomic background. In addition, they would grow as teacher leaders and stay longer in the teaching profession. We realized then that we could build a program in which we would carefully select expert teachers and provide them with rigorous training that would prepare them to mentor new teachers, building on the teachers' existing knowledge and enhancing it enough so that they would help their students learn better and feel competent and confident in their teaching. Thirteen years later, the New Teacher Center (NTC) reaches tens of thousands of teachers across the country and nearly two million students. Not only do we help new teachers become excellent at their profession, but we also build the human capital capacity in districts and states: the new teachers become more effective and stay in the classroom longer and the mentor teachers hone their expert practice even more, often becoming school and district leaders later on.

My dream was that in addition to helping ensure that every student has a great teacher, we would some-day influence the national dialogue and national policy on mentoring all new teachers during their induction years. Now, our influence has been spreading throughout the United States in different districts with varying contexts. The NTC has helped the field understand the importance of induction, the role of the mentor, and how to create strong, instructional mentoring programs that help new teachers become excellent teachers for their students.

In this process, we have learned a lot, too. Through our work, we have learned how to listen carefully and collaborate in ways that can help new teachers across the country improve student achievement in their classrooms. We have conducted a number of studies comparing new teachers with and without mentors to discover the impact on student achievement. And the evidence (including

Fletcher, Strong, and Villar, 2008) has shown that those mentored by the New Teacher Center have done better than those who weren't mentored.

This work is about ordinary people doing extraordinary things. Teaching new teachers is a relatively new idea that builds human capital. Mentors who learn to do this work are making an important contribution not just with their mentees, but also by helping to develop the professionalization of teaching.

We have learned that mentor preparation and continual learning is an important part of the mentor's education as well. Mentor forums are opportunities for the professional development of mentors because they get exposure to different kinds of problems and ways to solve them. Learning for mentors is as important as learning for new teachers.

This book couldn't come at a better time. Mentoring is now a part of the national dialogue on education. Numerous districts have found that they can accelerate teacher effectiveness and improve student learning when their teachers have been mentored through the New Teacher Center model. To be a good mentor and a good leader, mentors must learn how to negotiate their way through many different cultures: getting to know the teacher culture, working with principals, figuring out how to approach their mentees, and more. Navigating these tensions and learning from them is what this book is about. Its importance lies in giving us a deeper picture of the life and learning of mentors—important knowledge that we can use in building a cadre of mentor teacher leaders.

Reference

Fletcher, S., Strong, M., & Villar, A. (2008). An investigation of the effects of variations in mentor-based induction on the performance of students in California. *Teachers College Record, 110*(8), 2271–2289.

September 2011

Ellen Moir
Chief Executive Officer
New Teacher Center
Santa Cruz, California

PREFACE

Many books have been written about mentors and how they work. Some give advice, some describe the different contexts in which mentors work, some give specifics on how to mentor successfully.

This book attempts to add to the literature by describing the tensions and dilemmas that mentors face and how they go about negotiating a position and a way of operating in different contexts to help the novice teacher. In the process, the mentors learn to refine their skills and abilities.

This book has been a labor of love. For Ann it is a fulfillment of a long-term passion — figuring out how to get teacher leaders to write about how they are learning and the knowledge they are accruing. This is knowledge from practice that can only be mined by helping (in this case) mentors to write their own story. Susan sat with mentors for the purpose of learning about their experiences annually for four years and observed how mentors perceive the work of mentoring. By not trying to document the quality or impact of their mentoring, the refreshing focus was simply to encourage mentors to articulate the meaningful and challenging aspects of their work and the ways in which they deal with these challenges.

Having spent over twenty-five years working with mentors from across the country, Janet found this project to be a celebration of her mentor colleagues' knowledge, experience, passion, and wisdom. Facilitating writing retreats, stepping back from and distilling the mentors' collective learnings, and helping to give shape to their tensions was an incredible learning experience. And from that experience, we developed even greater respect and admiration for these on-the-ground teachers of teachers who are working with great dedication to improve the quality of teaching and student learning on a daily basis.

The book takes as its starting point a developmental look at the first two sites where mentors developed their roles over a four-year period. Analyzing the interview data uncovered the tensions of mentoring. Good induction programs clearly support not only the growth of beginning teachers but also the growth of those who mentor. The table in the Appendix was developed from what mentors said about their ongoing skill and knowledge growth over the three years that they were mentored. The table suggests broad areas in which mentors develop and issues that they generally face as first-, second-, and third-year mentors.

The book also includes vignettes, actual stories of how mentors struggle with new contexts, a new sense of identity, the ability to advance teacher growth, and how leadership develops between a mentor and mentee.

The stories are heroic and heartrending, dramatic and disturbing. We learn about the everyday foibles of the human condition and how different schools present different problems to solve for the mentor. We see all kinds of mentees, the reluctant and the eager, the stubborn and the stars — all engaged in one of the most complicated jobs we know — learning to teach.

Currently in the United States some teachers come from teacher education programs where they have had time and sometimes experience in teaching, but there are also people who have switched careers from other occupations to education. Some of the novice teachers have had a summer program of five weeks or less and now find themselves teaching high school students in very challenging schools. In any of these situations, the mentor must figure out how to approach the new teacher, how to work with experienced teachers, and how to connect to the principal and other leadership in the school. All of the mentors in this book are participants in the New Teacher Center — perhaps the best-known mentoring program in the country — a group that is more than two decades old and takes seriously the fact that mentors need professional development to assume their new jobs effectively.

Read on. Join with the mentors as they figure out how to approach their new school cultures and their mentees and listen to their experiences as they lay bare the tensions they face, their heartaches, and their stunning successes.

Ann Lieberman, Susan Hanson, Janet Gless

ACKNOWLEDGMENTS

This book could not exist without the thoughtful mentors who reflected on their mentoring and shared some of their most personally challenging experiences with us.

First, we want to acknowledge the support of Ellen Moir, chief executive officer of the New Teacher Center, who inspired and encouraged a longitudinal investigation of how mentoring supports the professional growth of veteran teachers.

We would like to acknowledge the mentors in Durham, North Carolina, and Boston, Massachusetts, who annually for four years talked candidly to Susan about their personal development as mentors and the challenges they faced each year. Pseudonyms are used in this book to protect the anonymity of those interviewed. We also want to acknowledge the mentors who came from several different sites and willingly participated and learned how to write about their mentor learning and helped us see the inside of mentor's lives. The Flora

Foundation supported this effort and was led by Janet and Ann. Janet, Susan, and the mentors in the Writing Collaborative are especially grateful for the expertise and advice of Ann Lieberman, whose vision, support, and mentoring carried this book to fruition.

ABOUT THE AUTHORS

Ann Lieberman is an emeritus professor from Teachers College, Columbia University. She was a senior scholar at the Carnegie Foundation for the Advancement of Teaching and is currently a senior scholar at Stanford University. Her many books and articles have been used by schools and universities alike. She has somehow fashioned a way to be a scholar and activist, practitioner and theoretician.

Susan Hanson, PhD, is a senior researcher at the New Teacher Center specializing in qualitative methods of program evaluation regarding teaching and learning. She has authored book chapters and journal articles and has presented at conferences on mentor development and the impact of mentoring on mentors. Specializing in the use of qualitative methodology to capture and understand K–12 schools, Dr. Hanson consults for foundations and previously worked at SRI and WestEd.

Janet Gless is one of the founders of the New Teacher Center. She is a former classroom teacher, mentor, program coordinator, and professional developer. Janet has authored many articles and book chapters on instructional mentoring and induction as well as a range of professional development courses for mentors and program leaders.

MENTORING TEACHERS

INTRODUCTION

In Part One we describe first the five major tensions that we found in a four-year interview study of mentors as they developed in one site as part of the New Teacher Center. This gave us enough data to agree on the following tensions. We then show more graphically what mentors in other sites describe as they write their own experiences about how they negotiate these tensions in different contexts. This will help mentors see the particulars of these tensions and how people develop and grow as mentors.

The five major tensions that we found in our analysis are as follows:

Tension One: Building a new identity

Tension Two: Developing trusting relationships

Tension Three: Accelerating teacher development

Tension Four: Mentoring in challenging contexts

Tension Five: Learning leadership skills

Building a New Identity

Mentors are most often chosen because they have shown excellence in their teaching. People have confidence that they know what they are doing and that they have learned over the years how to teach well, how to facilitate learning in students, have amassed a repertoire of teaching skills that they have reflected on, and are facilitative in nature. When they become mentors, many of them feel that somehow they have lost their teacher identity and they don't know how or why, but somehow there are a host of different expectations of them. Mentors must deal with the differing expectations of being an "expert" and they need to adapt quickly to different cultures. Many feel the unease and insecurity with a new role as they struggle for a new way to be. Somehow they must find the right balance between being open to new knowledge and keeping the knowledge that they have acquired as a teacher of students as they become a teacher of teachers. This unease with their identity and finding a new one takes time.

Developing Trusting Relationships

Teachers, when entering a new school culture, must learn quickly to understand the norms and values of the school. These cultural markers are important because understanding them can help new teachers to join the existing school community and clarifies the new school's potential influences—both negative and positive. Principals, veteran teachers, and other personnel in the school all represent potential partners or problems for the new teacher and therefore the mentor. Part of a mentor's role is to learn the new culture and help the mentee survive and thrive. Mentors often find themselves called on to support their mentees in light of fast-changing situations and pressures in this era of reform. Because most mentors work in several different schools, they must learn quickly how they can play a supportive role for their many mentees as they learn to teach.

Accelerating Teacher Development

Perhaps the most difficult job of all is helping novice teachers improve so that they can feel and actually facilitate success with students. Mentors find themselves involved with a central tension—that of providing emotional support and building a trusting relationship with a mentee and at the same time focusing on instructional content that improves the pedagogy of the new teacher. Which comes first? Making friends or improving one's teaching ability? How does one find a way into relationship building and teacher growth at a time when most mentees are suffering from not knowing how to teach and often feel vulnerable toward others who see their weaknesses. How can mentors do all this and in what order should mentors approach mentees as collaborators, learners, and potential partners in teaching. In negotiating this tension, mentors learn how to approach mentees, where to start, how to be flexible, and how to take steps that help the mentee become a full-fledged teacher by facilitating reflection about their developing practice. Because people are so different, no lists or standards exist to teach mentors how to approach novice teachers and how to help them enhance their pedagogy while at the same time develop a trusting and collaborative relationship. And what further complicates matters is that many contexts are so difficult in and of themselves.

Mentoring in Challenging Contexts

Many mentors find themselves in schools where there are mandates that limit pedagogical strategies that they deem important. They are confronted with having to figure out how to help novices deal with the mandates and at the same time how to learn pedagogical strategies that strengthen their teaching skills and abilities. Sometimes the climate in schools is such that impediments of all kinds affect the novice teacher and, in turn, the mentor. There are times when a mentor must take on novice teachers teaching a subject for which mentors have had limited experience. What do the mentors do? How can they be of value? At other times, mentors must learn how to work in contexts for which they have had limited experience, where norms of behavior are foreign to them, and where the leadership is sometimes challenging to them or to their mentees. How do mentors learn in these circumstances? What do they learn? How do these circumstances affect the mentor-mentee relationship?

Learning Leadership Skills

Although mentors may not think of themselves as leaders, they need to realize that their position requires brokering resources, advocating for social justice, supporting mentees when they are being wronged by the system or the culture, negotiating a position that helps the mentees learn despite difficult environments, and learning to balance what they can and cannot influence. Mentors learn that creating collaborative communities of practice for their mentees is a form of leadership. These skills and abilities to support, organize, collaborate, negotiate, and advocate are all aspects of leadership — often learned in the act of mentoring in different contexts, grade levels, and different subject areas.

PART ONE

The Tensions of Mentoring

TENSION ONE
Building a New Identity

·TENSION TWO·
Developing Trusting Relationships

·TENSION THREE·
Accelerating Teacher Development

·TENSION FOUR·
Mentoring in Challenging Contexts

·TENSION FIVE·
Learning Leadership Skills

TENSION·ONE

Building
a New Identity

*N*ew mentors gather at their first training session
excited and eager to learn more about their new
role. They have agreed to step away from their comfortable
past as successful, well-respected classroom teachers in a
school with familiar faces and ways of working to take
on new responsibilities supporting novice teachers in a
variety of schools. Although excited about the opportunity,
mentors, who are generally mid-career teachers, have only
a cursory understanding of what their new role as full-time
mentors really will entail.

Being selected as a mentor is public acknowledgment
that one is an excellent teacher with the potential to support
novice teachers. Practically overnight new mentors gain
the status of being a teacher of teachers with high expectations that they have the skills necessary to transmit their
knowledge and classroom expertise to novice teachers.

By the end of their first school year, mentors share that the job of teacher mentor is much more complex and challenging than they had imagined and the transition to being an outsider in school(s) was more difficult than anticipated. Similar to teaching, they had been thrown into all the responsibilities that the work entails, and with time and experience they gained a deeper understanding of the complexity of the task. Mentors know they are giving up working with children to work with novice teachers, but they don't always realize how significant the changes are on a personal level as they work in a variety of school settings with a variety of adults in their new status as "mentor teacher."

> Within the first two months I thought I would never be the same teacher again. I really feel that rather profoundly.... There is so much more to it—the way that you carry yourself matters, the way that you attend meetings.
>
> —JENNY

> This [first] year it's been very much about learning the culture of the school and the other people in the school; kind of letting them get a feel for me and not really knowing what was expected and acceptable when you're coming in as an outsider.
>
> —DAVID

The adjustment to their new role begins with each mentor's entry into a school or schools where their thirteen to twenty mentees work. Their identity of having a home base is lost unless they work in a school that has a large number of new teachers. Mentors enter as outsiders and draw on their social skills to introduce themselves and establish new relationships. Context really matters. At some schools, they are made to feel welcome by the principal and treated as part of the staff; in other schools, mentors find that feeling welcome or even having administrators and veteran teachers understand the value of their work cannot be taken for granted. Here are some examples of challenges mentors shared in connection with entry into their assigned schools:

I had a voice and respect at the school where I taught. Now I don't.

We're not always made to feel welcome.

I am selling the value of the program at my school.

Learning to navigate through appropriate channels has been a problem.

Not having a space of my own to hang my coat or keep papers is difficult.

Mentors see themselves first and foremost as a classroom teacher of children, and it takes time to transition to seeing themselves as a mentor or teacher of teachers.

I often felt like a fish out of water as I navigated a new system, new position, and working with teachers in areas that were outside of my comfort level. Not only was I learning a new role but also in a very different context than I was used to. I was learning how to use the FAS [formative assessment system] tools, build relationships with teachers in several different schools, learn each school's focus and mission, and develop relationships with building administrators without breaking confidentiality.... I felt as though I needed to have all the answers when in actuality I had very few.

—MARY

Over the past twelve years I've observed that a good majority of classroom teachers who stay in the profession for an extended period of time reach a state of proficiency and confidence in their practice that allows them to quickly adapt to the variety of challenges and demands in public education. Years of experience using both successful and unsuccessful teaching strategies and techniques build up a "cache" of confidence in knowing what will impact student achievement. This can-do confident attitude promotes effective teacher leadership across a campus. However, stepping out of the classroom teacher role and into the mentor teacher role can erode this confidence. You move from being an experienced master of your craft to the unknown realm of guiding and instructing fellow teachers.

—BECKY

In adjusting to my new role as a mentor, I underwent a very difficult shift in identity. In my role as a classroom teacher I was used to being in the role of Mr. Winstead to my students, who saw elements of my personality and life in measured, appropriate pieces.... As John, my colleagues got to know all about me, my life, my feelings on topics, and my likes and dislikes, all things that happen in typical interactions amongst coworkers and friends. As a mentor, I knew that things would have to change, but I was unprepared for how much of a new identity I would have to take on.

When you're having a bad day as a classroom teacher, you can turn to your colleagues, answer the "How are you doing?" question honestly, and just vent for a bit. I found, during my first year as a mentor, that my day and my feelings about how things were for me were secondary to the needs/feelings/thoughts of my teachers, as it should be when they are in crisis or just want to talk, celebrate, etc. That was fine because my work focused on their needs and their growth, but I couldn't help feeling that I was disconnected from the context in which I was working. I felt that I needed to wear a mask to go with this new identity of "everyman," someone who was whatever that person needed me to be at that moment.

—JOHN

By the end of the second year, mentors have worked with many more novice teachers, are more proficient at their job, and more comfortable in their role. Some remarked as follows:

> I didn't know what I didn't know last year! Even though I'm better at it, it's harder because I have more awareness of what's going on. We've had more training, which included issues of equity, ESL learners, and EC [early childhood] learners. I'm learning more about what's going on and I'm finding it's more complex.
>
> —PAUL

> I'm much less intimidated about walking into their classrooms this year than I was last year. I have more knowledge of what my role really is and what's possible in my role, And, I know more of the faculty at both schools than I did last year and have learned the dynamics a little bit.
>
> —JENNY

After mentors feel comfortable with their new identity as a "new teacher mentor," they still run into many situations in which they wonder, "What's my role in this situation? How should I behave? What's my responsibility under these circumstances?" Mentors must make judgments regarding how to behave in a variety of unanticipated situations. The dilemmas and challenges they face represent the typical tensions of mentoring. Following are a few examples of the issues mentors confront. Some of the issues cross over with themes covered in other chapters and will be discussed in more detail later.

What's my role with the principal? Sometimes principals want to put us to work on their agenda and I need to maintain confidentiality.

People have high expectations for what we produce out of the teachers we mentor. What's my role and responsibility when a teacher is not performing adequately and is not following my suggestions?

I find it challenging to have to sit quietly and be an observer rather than jump in and fix things.... Knowing that I have good skills as a teacher ... to what extent can I make sure students receive good teaching?

Working with third years who think they are fine and don't recognize that they still have areas in which they need help with.... How do I help them in a professional way?

Standing on the outside and looking in is hard.... I see site-based decisions that take time away from important things. I see all the things that teachers have to put up with. What role can I play to help conditions improve?

Working in new schools, mentoring new teachers, and participating in sustained mentor training help mentors shift their perspective from being a classroom teacher to that of an educator with a broader perspective. What several mentors described as gaining a "global" perspective has implications for their vision of good schools, good teaching, and how to help teachers improve their practice.

Becoming a mentor expands the vision of midcareer teachers as to how they can contribute to improving schools and the teaching profession.

> Being able to see it from the teachers' perspective, to be able to see it from the administrators' perspectives, and to be able to see it from the principal's perspective, which is different from the administrators' perspectives as well as the other people in the building that support staff that's there. That has been one of my hugest learnings this year.
>
> —MELISSA

The shift from having the perspective of a classroom teacher to that of an educator was transformational for many mentors and has implications for how they work with other educators and view the profession of teaching.

> The biggest insight that I gained is having this global perspective.... Whereas as a teacher I was quite happy to just close my door and be in my room because I was good at it and my kids were good at it in my room and so it was easy to just think, "All you other people figure out how to get it good in your room." That's different for me now. It's really changed the way I look at education.
>
> —NANCY

Mentors are first and foremost experienced teachers, some of whom had taught in only one school prior to their being selected as a district mentor. Their experience as mentors broadens their understanding of teaching and learning in different school cultures. As principals and veteran teachers see the value of their support to new teachers, and mentors become more knowledgeable and comfortable in their role, mentors become more confident and able to support teachers in more ways. As mentors move from being a first-year mentor, a second-year mentor, and then a third-year mentor, their growing experiences support an increasing number of beginning teachers with different strengths and needs and increases their understanding of how they can influence the quality of teaching across school contexts and working conditions. Building one's identity and skills as a mentor is a developmental process rather than a static occurrence.

·TENSION ONE·

Building a New Identity

TENSION TWO

Developing Trusting Relationships

·TENSION THREE·

Accelerating Teacher Development

·TENSION FOUR·

Mentoring in Challenging Contexts

·TENSION FIVE·

Learning Leadership Skills

TENSION · TWO

Developing Trusting Relationships

*M*ost mentors come from schools in which they are well respected and have developed trusting relationships with members of the school community, students, colleagues, and their administrator. When mentors come to new schools, they must establish the same kind of trusting relationships that they have had in their own schools. This is not always easy!

When teachers assume their new role as mentors, they may not realize how profoundly their relationships with coworkers will change. Their new job requires building and maintaining relationships differently than they had become accustomed to as a classroom teacher. With students, teachers, administrators, and resource teachers, mentors must figure out how to work as an outsider working on the inside. Now their colleagues with whom to confide are mentors like themselves, learning to negotiate many new situations and build trusting relationships essential to their success supporting new teachers.

Building relationships as a mentor involves many changes and unforeseen challenges. Even the most basic change of switching from working with children to working with adults can be an adjustment for teachers. During her first year of mentoring, Candace explained:

> You're in the classroom for so long and you kind of have a groove with kids and you get that kind of perspective and then shifting gears to learning how to interact with adults. . . . With other teachers when you're teaching, you're in the same boat and you talk in the hallway and sometimes socialize. This working with adults is an interesting area to develop. Some days I wish I had my teenagers back.
>
> —CANDACE

Some mentors had not really thought about how building relationships with people other than beginning teachers was going to be an important part of their new job. They were surprised at how awkward it could be to initiate conversations in a new school with teachers and administrators, especially when it's common to feel as if you need to live up to the status of your new "mentor" title. It takes careful consideration to know what to say to people you have never met to assure them you are approachable and there to be supportive. It is one thing to start a conversation with a new teacher but it can take courage to talk to principals as colleagues when you are accustomed to talking to them as a classroom teacher. One teacher admitted,

> [At first], I kept my head down and tried to avoid administrative confrontations at all costs unless I had some candy or chocolate to break the ice. I was so afraid that principals would ask questions that I couldn't answer about the program or about my beginning teachers. I made it through that first year feeling great about the relationships that I had built.... I set a goal my second year to increase my interactions with principals.
>
> I think in the beginning it was a push for me to make myself approach principals, but I realize that it's a really necessary part of my job.
>
> —JENNY

The relationship between mentors and administrators is crucial. The tension between facilitative coaching and supervisoral feedback in K–12 education can make the principal-mentor partnership challenging in a number of ways. Mentors should receive professional support in how to develop relationships with administrators and communicate the importance of confidentiality in their role as trusted advisors to their mentees. Maintaining confidentiality while developing a partnership with administrators is tricky. One mentor talked about how her principal initially preferred to have no contact with her as a way to maintain confidentiality but then it didn't help him understand what the mentor did that was useful at his school. It took a variety of attempts by the mentor to make headway:

> When I tried to meet with my principal in the past he told me that he wanted me to speak to him through a different person who is no longer at the school.... Next I tried to meet with an assistant principal. He didn't show up to four meetings.

The mentor, concerned that there seemed to be a lot of mystery around why she was really placed in the low-performing high school, was intent to make her usefulness understood and establish trust. When she finally got to meet with the principal, she shared an example of what she had recently done for a teacher:

> I showed one of my favorite tools to the principal. It's making a map of the classroom and making a map of what's actually happening. This particular time there was a lot of talking during the lesson. He was shocked by the lack of student engagement that the maps showed. He doesn't see things like that so he found it very interesting.

Using real data demonstrated a concrete way that the mentor could provide informed feedback to a teacher who showed a need for improvement. And, it led to a discussion about ways that such a tool could have broader application at the school. This was one way that the mentor was able to overcome her challenge of getting others to understand what she did at their school behind closed doors working with mentees. Being valued as a mentor at a school takes extra work and time in some schools. Subsequently, she shared the following:

> I think that because I've been there for three years they are slowly getting it. I mean, initially they saw me as a mole.... And now I think they see me as somebody who helps teachers.

There are important reasons for other teachers to understand the mentor's role and potential consequences if they do not. Mentors come to understand that their role includes relationship building at their schools.

> I work very hard on making sure that the perception of those who don't work with me one-on-one is accurate.... I don't view my role as just serving the beginning teachers. I have to get the advanced teachers on board so that the perception of my role is pervasive. Because if I have advanced teachers looking at what I do and snickering about it, and I have beginning teachers hearing that when I'm not around, that works against what I'm doing. So I'm trying to indoctrinate the role from the principal down. That means going to parent meetings, that means going to team-level meetings, and going to after-school meetings.

Veteran teachers, working side by side with beginning teachers, strongly influence the school culture. Teacher attitudes and ways of being become a concern to mentors when they see how they contribute to the culture in which their mentees work.

> In my school, there's an all-or-nothing feel with how the veterans treat the new teachers. Either they're one hundred percent supportive and wonderful or they're the worst influences you could put in a school for a teacher. How do I either protect the new teachers from these negative veteran teachers or how do I get the veteran teachers to be more positive role models or at least not be detrimental? Sometimes they say really snarky things in the copy room and just cast a pall over the attitude of some of the new teachers. Then they act grumpy and like they've been doing this forever, even though they're just twenty-two! . . . I don't know whether I need to work more with the ILTs [initially licensed teachers] or work more within the school to keep that from happening.
>
> —DAVID

Mentors struggle with whether and how to help improve the school culture. In some schools, they inadvertently find themselves trying to help to develop a supportive school culture that will nourish their mentee's spirit rather than diminish it. Attending grade level or department meetings provides a good vehicle for mentors to observe teachers working together. As outsiders, just figuring out how to behave in one's role as a mentor at a teacher meeting takes consideration. Here's how one new teacher mentor talked about trying to gain trust and respect among several teachers in her new role:

> In some cases, I attend PLC [professional learning community] meetings with my ILTs. At first I rarely spoke. In fact, I only spoke when a question was phrased, "Does anybody know how to ____?" After a few successes, more teachers realized that I knew what I was talking about. At those grade levels, I am now included in discussions and frequently asked questions by ILTs and veterans. However, I am still not welcome at other meetings.
>
> —BRENDA

The context of each school is different and it can be enormously stressful for mentors who work in a few schools to determine actual rules from unspoken rules and to learn to work within a variety of school cultures simultaneously.

Part of assuming a new role requires understanding one's relationship not only to principals and other veteran teachers but also to one's mentees. Interacting with beginning teachers as a mentor is pretty clear but even it can be perplexing. Mentors are credentialed teachers—and, having just left classroom teaching, this is often how they first and foremost still see themselves. Mentors identify with other teachers and find it easy to be collegial with them. This can create a dilemma for mentors working with mentees who are also credentialed teachers. Here is how John explained this common struggle involving relationships with mentees:

> I feared getting too close, too personal with my teachers, concerned that I would find it hard to mentor them if they were struggling [and] if I liked them so much as people or that I would appear to be favoring one over another.
>
> —JOHN

Mentors, as teachers of teachers, spend most of their time working with their mentees. When teachers take breaks at lunch from their students, they can talk with other teachers, but for mentors there are usually no other true colleagues to talk with at school. Mentees and mentors are all adults but they are not colleagues in the way that mentors are with other mentors.

Mentors and principals must to learn to work together as coleaders for teacher learning without breaching mentor-teacher confidentiality. As gatekeepers to teacher retention and tenure, helping principals truly support beginning teachers and encouraging their growth is an important aspect of mentor work. Mentors tell stories of working for months to help a principal differentiate between what is the mentor's role in supporting beginning teachers and what is the principal's role.

> The principals may sometimes ask us more than we should be telling them and so I tend to develop a repertoire of answers around what they want to know.... We're there to help the beginning

teachers. I don't believe in getting mixed up in building politics or serving on any committees in any building we're in because then your role is compromised. We do not report to principals, but sometimes principals see an extra body in their building and they want to put you to work right away. I think we have to be really cautious about that.

—NANCY

How principals deal with novice teachers not performing as well as expected can pose several problems for mentors. In the best of cases, mentors help the teacher in question to work on particular areas mutually identified for improvement. In other cases, they must help a mentee reach particular goals that they may not consider as important as others, but they are school goals. Or, in the most difficult cases, mentors must encourage the mentee to use particular strategies that they may not think are most appropriate, such as scripted lessons. Here is one example of how a mentor used her principal's focus on test scores to help a teacher progress satisfactorily in his eyes:

A challenging situation that one of my teachers faced was trying to navigate the principal's vision and philosophy of teaching with her own. She was organized, diligent in planning, assessing, scaffolding the work, and having her students work in collaborative teams. But the work didn't show

31

in student test scores. It was difficult for me to support this teacher through her trying to do a good teaching job, and at the same time do what the principal expected. There was evidence of growth with her students (as she tried to make up for a weak background in math). But to make matters worse, the principal handed her an action plan in the hall between classes that stated that she needed to raise test scores or she would not be renewed.... I helped her create some goals for her teaching that she could share with the principal. We analyzed data and created some easy formative assessments.... Somehow she needed to find a balance between what she felt was right for her students and what her principal expected. They were not always the same.

—DANIEL

Mentors must learn not only to navigate their relationship with principals, but they often also find themselves trying to improve communication between the principal and beginning teachers. Mentors tell stories about challenging situations in which a mentee has a strained relationship with the principal and does not feel supported by him or her. Mentors may go to great efforts trying to help the teacher be seen in a better light. In other cases, principals suggest to mentors that the mentee is not likely to get his or her contract renewed.

I had a principal who wanted me to tell the new teacher that she was going to rescind her letter of reasonable assurance next summer and I said, "I really think you need to have that conversation." She wanted me to do the dirty work.

—NANCY

It's essential that mentors be aware of situations early enough so they can work with the beginning teacher to improve the skills in which the principal has concern, along with the mentee's relationship with the principal. Otherwise, tensions escalate for the mentor and the mentee.

The principal really doesn't have any problem so much with what the beginning teacher is doing in the classroom. He just says she's "not a good fit." He told her that she isn't being rehired. But he never said, "Maybe you could work on this." She [my mentee] was shocked and hurt. And, he lied to her about the reason and said it was budget cuts. It made me feel powerless. I really respect what she does and I really respect the principal, too! I respect both of their positions and I try not to pick one as right or wrong because he has to run that school. And he has to decide what works for his team. But I also feel that if I'm going to be in a place [this school] for ten months, let me know if there are things that I can address.

—SANDRA

Through building relationships at a school, mentors can positively influence how administrators, veteran teachers, and resource teachers view and behave with new teachers. In heartwarming cases, mentors tell of people at a school who thought a particular teacher would not make it and came around to see that that with time and support, teachers can blossom and become a model for effective teaching.

·TENSION ONE·
Building a New Identity

·TENSION TWO·
Developing Trusting Relationships

TENSION THREE
Accelerating Teacher Development

·TENSION FOUR·
Mentoring in Challenging Contexts

·TENSION FIVE·
Learning Leadership Skills

TENSION ' THREE

Accelerating Teacher Development

O ne of the centerpieces of the mentor-mentee relationship turns out to be one of the biggest sources of tension for the mentor and perhaps for the mentee as well. Some of the important questions to consider include the following:

- How should the mentee be approached and helped?

- Is it more important to build a relationship and then work on the teaching practice?

- What do you do when the students are climbing the walls and this is your first connection to the mentee?

- How do you determine when to intervene or when to wait?

- Is classroom management always the right place to start?

- How do you learn how to build on what your mentee already knows?

- How do you learn timing and good approaches to a mentee who needs a lot of help?

These are all legitimate worries of mentors, particularly those who are just in their beginning years.

Novice teachers, however, are often reluctant to admit their troubles or sometimes accept a mentor's help or support. Somehow new teachers *feel* that they should know everything about how to teach regardless of the school, student neighborhood, or subject area. Although they can use some support, some are reluctant to admit they need it. Others are open and may ask for help, but the newly minted mentor might not know where to start. These reflect the tensions of a mentee, but discovering their cause is also the bedrock on which mentors learn just exactly when and in what way to intervene. As you will see in the following mentor quotes, the struggle to understand and act on the intricacies involved in building relationships and helping new teachers improve their practice is part of what it means to become a good and sensitive mentor. And it is in the struggle to know how, when, and in what manner to help or intervene that mentors learn their trade.

> I think the hardest thing is in your first or second year of mentoring that you really want to show these teachers that you can help them, and that sort of is in direct conflict with relationship build-ing and taking a slow approach that I think a lot of

these new teachers need in order to feel comfortable with you.

—MEGAN

Learning to trust and empower, rather than swoop in and try to fix everything, is hard. A particular teacher may not be ready or able to implement a new strategy or change a dynamic in his or her classroom at a given moment. I have had to learn to sit with my own feelings of frustration and urgency and redirect my energy toward supporting that teacher in believing in his or her own capacity, regardless of the choices of that moment.

—KATIE

The new teachers look at me as if I know all the answers! Flattering yet unnerving. Will I be able to help them when the time comes?

—AMY

There is so much to learn as a beginning mentor that it is not surprising that mentors don't get it all right the first time around; it takes time to figure it out. There is not only the mentee to worry about but also the culture of the school and building trusting relationships with the administrative leadership and veteran teachers.

Finding the right entry point can be difficult; however, I have learned that timing is everything and knowing the person's needs is essential.

—SOPHIA

When veteran teachers are mediocre at best, the bar is not set very high. The veteran teachers are setting the tone and some of the mentees accept this as the way it is and the way it should be. This is quite a mentoring challenge.

—BRENDA

Sometimes pacing guides and scripted curriculum make it hard for mentors to find a place where they can be helpful in moving a teacher's practice forward.

My challenge as a mentor has been helping my teachers find ways to teach background knowledge and vocabulary needed to access the curriculum (scaffolding) while teaching the curriculum under time constraints and pacing guides set forth by the district.

—BRENDA

Some mentors, despite their own good education, learn to work with mentees through the experience of actually facing different teaching and learning problems. In the process they develop a repertoire and a way of working, each time learning more about how to help mentees where it matters.

I was able to create meaningful, trusting relationships with teachers who had a variety of needs. I met them where they were and was accessible on their terms. By making myself available to each teacher, but not pushing too hard at first, I was able to earn their trust and move on to have responsive coaching interactions throughout the year. My colleagues saw improvements in their classrooms and were excited to have meetings with me.

—CINDY

In my nine visits and classroom observations, I never witnessed my beginning teacher integrating activities in the classroom that fully engaged students, introduced anything to get them out of their seats, or had them take responsibility for their own learning. Despite my knowledge of how an engaged class should behave, too much time had passed before I intervened on behalf of those bored students.

My conversation opened the beginning teacher's mind to new ideas and a chance to see the class from the students' seat. Would you want to be in your class? It is easy to tell mentors to intervene, but it's tougher to do it. My beginning teacher has started to move in the right direction, but next time the urgency won't let me be so subtle.

—KATIE

We learn that mentoring teachers is in some ways like teaching students. You can know a great deal, but when it

41

comes to teaching the particulars there is a great deal to be learned through the experience of actually having to teach novice teachers. You learn when to step in and when to be silent, when to build trust, or when to focus on bettering teaching practice.

·TENSION ONE·
Building a New Identity

·TENSION TWO·
Developing Trusting Relationships

·TENSION THREE·
Accelerating Teacher Development

TENSION FOUR
Mentoring in Challenging Contexts

·TENSION FIVE·
Learning Leadership Skills

TENSION ' FOUR

Mentoring in Challenging Contexts

*M*entors who are responsible for a number of novice teachers often find themselves in school contexts that prove to be very challenging. The reasons are varied, but they all cause disruption in the work and tension in the job and a necessary focus on how to negotiate situations that are often new and complicated.

It's challenging to keep the teachers motivated and uplifted when the administration comes behind me and tears them down.

—JOLIE

Mentors get to see the "dirty underbelly of education." Sometimes teachers demean their students. Sometimes administrators yell injustices. It takes talent to navigate mentoring in these situations. You need to learn to ask questions and figure out who the support people are. The more important thing for me was returning to the standards and having faith that the novice teachers can learn how to be professional and maintain a classroom.

—DELLA

One challenge I have faced as a mentor, particularly at low-performing schools, is working with beginning teachers on grade levels with ineffective veteran teachers. . . . At my lowest-performing school, I have dealt with all sorts of inappropriate treatment stemming from jealousy over test scores.

—BRENDA

Sometimes mentors find themselves in schools where there are mandates and scripts for *what* to teach and *how* to teach particular subjects. This puts mentors in a tough position because they are trying to build the novice teachers' confidence and at the same time give them strategies that enhance their pedagogy.

Working with scripted curricula and seeing lots of stressed-out teachers and administrators is difficult. Teachers focusing on test scores leads some administrators to rule with an iron fist—not really caring about the teachers as people. Having conferences with administrators who are treating teachers harshly, I let them know how this treatment is affecting the teachers.

—JOLIE

In other situations, the school climate is not conductive to being open to learning. New teachers struggle to find support and mentors must find ways of working when there is tension and conflict between their work and administrators who are giving a different message. Mentors can indeed support novices, but they have a difficult time fighting a climate of fear, despondency, anxiety, or constant pressure to raise test scores. Their goals as mentors are to facilitate new teacher strategies that build a foundation for learning to teach.

> Working with the administration was always a challenge for me at this particular school. The first two years I felt that things would change: the culture of the school would change, and the administration would become more supportive over time.
>
> But that did not happen. So this year when I took people in, I knew what they were going to face. After just a short time they became aware of what they had stepped into.... It was different because I felt very discouraged. I knew that I was taking people into a place that was going to be challenging for them.
>
> —LINDA

I have become aware of how vastly different cultures are in different schools. This can be enormously stressful as a mentor because it is sometimes difficult to determine actual rules from unspoken rules, and new people don't know whom to ask.

—BRENDA

Mentors sometimes find themselves in schools that feel entirely foreign to them. They have been hired because they have been outstanding teachers in particular subject areas but are placed in schools where they are expected to mentor teachers in subject areas about which they know very little.

I did everything in that interview to show proof of how effective I was as an upper grade language arts and social science teacher. There are only a few teaching contents in which I am comfortable putting myself in the role of "expert." Let's just say I felt like I was completely out of my league. I soon learned that it became a question of *how* they taught the topic.

—TARA

After spending a few days with each of two mentors, I knew that I was going to make it. They helped me understand immediately how I could help teachers in those classes in which I had absolutely no knowledge. The more you understand the purpose, the easier the job becomes. Within a month or so, I was very comfortable researching on the computer, and I began exploring opportunities for successes that were brand new to me, yes, even math, science, and Spanish.

—ANN

At times, mentors must learn that schools differ in the way they get things accomplished, the kinds of students and teachers they have, and the way the principal or leadership team works. Schools develop complicated cultures that mentors must understand. What goes on in one school is anathema to another.

> Serving teachers in a more peaceful and well-resourced part of the city, the experiences of my beginning teachers were somewhat foreign to me.... I had developed thoughtful ways to process death and tragedy into our writing and choice time activities, but I was somewhat inexperienced at community building without intense life tragedies to draw us together.
>
> —LIZ

When I was at Jordan, I taught AP level courses and also standard level courses. I saw students who were flying to Europe for spring break, then in the next class students who never left Durham. When I was sent to Southern High School I wasn't surprised that there were very poor students. I was happy to be there to work with students and help teachers prepare for the challenges of helping students who are not interested in learning. But

49

I am not happy now as the school is failing because the adults in the building aren't doing their job.

——JENNA

In this particular period of time, mentors often work in districts that are struggling with reduced budgets, laying off people, and generally trying to find ways to stay afloat. Mentors feel this strain as they work with teachers at the beginning of their careers but their futures may look dim.

> At the end of this school year, many beginning teachers were contacting me about losing their positions. Knowing that our school district was in financial straits, I expected to hear about job losses. Unfortunately, I was not expecting to have to offer encouraging words without any foreseeable solutions. I realized that I could review the tools we had learned together and prepare them for the many interviews that they would get.
>
> ——BETTY

These challenging contexts must somehow be handled by the mentors. As you will see, mentors find all kinds of personal and professional ways of supporting, sometimes protecting, and often negotiating their way through the thicket. In the process of being faced with all these challenges, some of which are the school's own making and sometimes reflect a mentor's lack of particular experience, mentors learn to seek help when they need it, broker for their mentees, adjust to new environments, and negotiate difficult school cultures using these experiences to grow and develop as leaders.

·TENSION ONE·
Building a New Identity

·TENSION TWO·
Developing Trusting Relationships

·TENSION THREE·
Accelerating Teacher Development

·TENSION FOUR·
Mentoring in Challenging Contexts

TENSION FIVE
Learning Leadership Skills

TENSION · FIVE

Learning Leadership Skills

*L*eadership skills to support, organize, collaborate, negotiate, and advocate are all abilities that mentors learn as part of their complex work with novice teachers. As mentors confront the four tensions of mentoring discussed in previous chapters—building a new identity, developing trusting relationships, accelerating teacher development, and mentoring in challenging contexts—they gain experience and learn valuable leadership skills.

Having an identity as a leader is influenced by one's past experience, and feeling like a leader doesn't simply happen on gaining the title of *mentor*. Mentors can comfortably explain how they help teachers improve their practice and how they can work with groups of teachers to learn new teaching strategies. But when asked, "What do you do as a leader?" they often pause and have difficulty explaining this integral aspect of mentoring.

Mentors, as respected classroom teachers, usually associate "leadership" experience with being on school or district leadership councils. To answer the question as to whether they are leaders, they list the planning groups, councils, and committees in which they have participated. Then they pause and add that as mentors they don't actually feel like leaders. In fact, as first-year mentors, they feel more like "newbies," having to prove themselves in places where they are not known. Here's how Jenna, at the end of her first year of mentoring, explained her situation:

> When other teachers respect what is going on in your classroom, they come to you for help. Last year when I was teaching at Somers high school, I had a lot of science teachers say, "I need help with this. Do you have resources for this?" I was a resource for a lot of teachers.... And as a mentor that's changed a little bit.... We're all brand new. At the science department at Hadden High School [my current school], I try to serve as a resource for them, but they don't really use me. So, my leadership in some areas has been diminished in terms of being a good science teacher with a lot of resources.
>
> —JENNA

Jenna knew she was a leader in her former position as an esteemed high school teacher but she didn't feel like a leader except when she convened her mentees and helped them. In weekly mentor meetings, Jenna was inspired by how much she could learn from listening and sharing with her new colleagues. As much as she appreciated being in this group, she could see that, relatively new to mentoring, she had a lot to learn.

So, how do mentors gain the leadership attributes that others recognize in them? As mentors shift from their core identification as strong classroom teachers with a respected voice in one school to that of a teacher mentor working in many school contexts, they encounter school, district, and certification issues affecting their mentees that can help expand their skill set. When mentors speak up or take action on behalf of their mentees, they gain valuable experience as change agents in a school setting. Jenna went on to explain:

> I'm learning a lot about even just the way that I am.... It wasn't important before because I was just a teacher. [Correction:] I wasn't just a teacher, I was a teacher. I operated in a much smaller world. My personality and way of being and the way that I operate is a major player now.... It is much easier to make people upset. So, I'm learning that when I do things, I need to think more systemically and not on such a limited level. I can't just think about how it affects my teachers directly; I need to figure out how it affects the department or the entire school. I have to have a more global perspective, and I learned that the hard way I guess is what I'm saying.
>
> —JENNA

Something as simple as brokering classroom textbooks or equipment for a new teacher can take up resources of a school department, creating resentment among other department members. Speaking up in a meeting in support of or against a particular way of teaching can inadvertently hurt relationships with teachers who were at a school long before the mentor.

Mentors tell stories of ways in which they stepped up to advocate for something they believed would benefit students. Sometimes mentors are not aware of how an administrator will react to actions they take to support beginning teachers. They may courageously try to fix a poor working condition or an injustice to a beginning teacher, only to have others respond negatively to their efforts. The tensions resulting from not seeing all issues beforehand come out in the individual stories told by mentors. Here's a brief story of how Jenna took initiative to assist some beginning teachers that was met with unanticipated repercussions for herself, but probably made her wiser as a leader:

> The beginning teachers had been promised payment for their teaching after hours. They weren't paid for six weeks and weren't sure that the payment was coming, so I helped them advocate for that.... I recently had a meeting with [the principal] because he was very, very upset with me about advocating for the teachers about the evening school.
>
> —JENNA

How do mentors remain true to fundamental principles of good practice and norms in a context that is antithetical to their beliefs? Mentors sometimes are pushed to develop leadership skills out of the school's need for more leadership supportive of developing teachers. They want to support schools where students and teachers can thrive. Mentors find themselves helping teachers navigate challenging district policies and practices—advocating for better working conditions and best teaching practices, fair and useful teacher evaluations, and fewer extra assignments for novice teachers. Stories of mentors going beyond their primary job of improving teacher practice to help new teachers advocate for themselves are examples of how mentors step up and exhibit leadership skills. Figuring out what is yours to influence and what is not with mentees, administrators, and other teachers regarding department or grade level practices can be a source of significant tension for mentors.

When asked about how mentoring contributes to leadership development, mentors reflect on and compare how they "used to be" as a teacher working with other teachers versus how they would behave now as a teacher if the same situation presented itself. Because they have been teachers, they can identify with the challenges that their mentees may face and hope to teach them to stand up for what they believe is best for students. Mentoring makes former teachers more equipped to be leaders in their schools and districts. In the following quote, a young mentor shares a personal story that provides an example of her growth in confidence to speak up:

> I was a person who felt very intimidated by the veteran teachers around me. If they were all doing this project, whether it was really grounded in the standard course of study, I felt like I had to sort of go along. I wasn't a person who would say, "Hey, this is not right, you know, let's try this." Now I think I would feel like I can't just go along with that. I know that's not what we need to be spending our time on. For my kids I need to be doing this. I think I would feel like I absolutely couldn't just go along with it. I would stand up for myself a little bit more.
>
> —JENNY

The knowledge and skills that experienced teachers potentially acquire as part of their mentor training and practice can be viewed as part of a career of continual professional growth. Following, we take a closer look at a few discussions with Jenny over a period of years to understand more concretely how being a mentor can have a profound impact on a teacher's leadership development.

For Jenny, working with principals provided opportunities and tensions that supported her leadership development in ways that even surprised her. The following excerpts from interviews with Jenny take us from her early reflections about working with principals to her thinking about her future role in schools.

Leadership is an area where I have had to really push myself. We have some professional opportunities coming up. One is to address the administrators at their summer retreat.... I feel very strongly about the relationship with the administration as being really crucial to this job. This is something I felt pretty passionate about, but it's a little nerve racking to think about doing that [presenting to the administrators]. I had to really push myself to apply for this opportunity!

When Jenny became a mentor, she was told that it would be for a fixed three-year term. She was thrilled to be selected as a mentor and anticipated returning to teaching after an enriching experience. However, after working as a full-time mentor, her vision of what she might do after mentoring greatly expanded, so much so that thinking about and making decisions about her career path became another unanticipated "tension" of mentoring.

It's been a really big decision for me, and it's really changed me.... There is something about this year and the ending of the training from the NTC that just sort of left me with a feeling that you have to take what you know now and do something with it.

To go back to the classroom is important; it's where the most important work is being done. So ironically, to come to the decision to go into administration, I struggled with it a lot, because I really do think we could facilitate a great change by going back into the classroom, especially by going back into some of the schools that we've seen struggling.

I've never considered myself someone who would go into administration, but I just found a lot of the systemic issues, a lot of the big issues that were dealt with in the inquiry process, were so inspiring.... They left me with a feeling of responsibility to do more; it really almost lit a fire under me.... I want to do it in a way that's like mentoring.... I really want to get away from the hierarchical structure where this is the leader of the school, because that's how I'm accustomed to seeing it done, and I think that's what made me feel like I would never go into administration, but I am now seeing the possibility for it to be done in a different way.

This story of one mentor's development is important not only because it shows how mentoring can transition into a career path to school leadership but also, most important, because of the type of leader Jenny wants to be. Similar to other mentors, Jenny used the tensions she confronted as a mentor to help her envision being a "transformational leader" who will promote the highest-quality classroom practice and support teacher growth in very different ways than most administrators are equipped to do.

The knowledge and skills that experienced teachers potentially acquire as part of their mentor training and practice can be viewed as part of a career path of continual professional growth, regardless of what mentors do after mentoring. Some mentors return to teaching and they too are forever changed by their mentoring experience. As Keith reflected on his journey, we gain some insight into how mentoring expands the identity of teachers into leaders:

> I don't think I can ever be just a teacher again. I'm not sure they'll know what they hired because I have the confidence to advocate for myself and for a department.... When I believe in something, I will fight for it.... I'm hoping the mentoring serves me well in having those fierce conversations and crucial conversations so that everybody gets what they want.
>
> —KEITH

As mentors deepen their coaching skills and gain broader experience working in schools, they gain confidence as teacher leaders, regardless of what particular role they go on to assume after mentoring. Mentors not only know how to support teaching practice, but with their enhanced skills and knowledge they can also be valuable assets to help leverage change in school systems.

> I'm seeing mentoring as more of a leadership role. For example, when I met the principal last year, he said, "I don't know what I'm going to do with you. I don't know what I'm supposed to do with you." When I was at the job fair this year [as a mentor], he came and found me and had me talk to people

he was interviewing.... That made me feel like he was accepting this position as valuable.

—GWEN

In this example, Gwen expresses an awareness of the mentor role as a leadership position. Gwen is more than a beginning teacher mentor. She is a teacher leader who is valued by her principal as an important member of the school community who helps to create a school culture where teachers are supported as professionals. As these mentors struggle for an identity, their leadership is being forged by the negotiation of the tensions they face as well as the successes they learn to internalize.

PART TWO

Stories of Mentoring

STORY ONE
The Waiting Place

STORY TWO
Fired, Hired, and Inspired

STORY THREE
Finding a Way

STORY FOUR
Savior, Friend, Mentor

The Waiting Place

In this poignant story of a career changer becoming a teacher, we watch the growing relationship between the mentor and her mentee. We see the consequences of the school context on the students, mentee, and mentor. We experience the mentor's skill in building a personal and professional relationship with the mentee. Fighting the effects of an unsupportive school, the mentor tries to help her mentee acquire teaching strategies that will help him succeed. Acts of kindness and sensitivity connect the mentor to her mentee, which assists in building a way to work together and move them both from "the waiting place."

The Waiting Place

by Leslie Baldacci

*I*n a large, turbulent urban school district with twelve thousand teachers, it is easy to blend unnoticed into a landscape of mediocrity. Some teachers spend their entire careers in what Dr. Seuss calls "the waiting place." It's a "most useless place" where people wait for things to happen instead of seizing the day and making things happen. It's a disempowered place.

That is where I met Mr. N at the start of his first full year teaching a split-grade class in a small neighborhood school in Chicago's South Side. The fact that I met him there is an admission that I, too, was in "the waiting place"—the common mentoring tension of not feeling worthy of the "expert" role.

I was an alternative certification career changer who survived two hellish first years. Despite four very good years after that, I had yet to forgive myself for my own first-year failings. I still bore scars of self-doubt from a culture of criticism and isolation that breaks so many new teachers. Mr. N was reliving my experience.

He had arrived midwinter the year before at the once-distinguished elementary school, now on academic probation. His classroom—in a mobile unit—was a bunker where he hid out with his twenty-two students. He did not respond to e-mails or return phone calls. (Another mentoring tension: the resistant teacher.) My first visit, therefore, was a surprise.

"You're visiting Mr. N?" the office clerk asked, one eyebrow up. A twitch at the side of her mouth suggested she had plenty to say but held back.

"I'll let him know you're here," she said, flipping the intercom switch.

"Yes," a tinny voice emerged from the static of classroom noise—children's voices, chairs scraping floor, bodies bumping desks.

"You have a visitor," the clerk announced.

"OK," came the weary reply.

I walked down two hallways, out the back door, across a parking lot, past a playground, and up the wooden ramp of the half-occupied, four-room mobile unit. The brown metal door was locked. Wire mesh over the small window rattled like a snare drum when I knocked. A face peered through before the door swung open.

"I'm a coach from the New Teacher Center," I said. "I'm here to see Mr. N."

"Good, he needs it," the security guard said, shaking her head in an "ain't it a shame" sort of way. Whatever professional restraint the clerk had shown in the office was not in effect at the outpost.

"He has no classroom management," the guard confided in a confidential tone, walking me the short distance to his door. "His kids can't even walk through the hallways."

Mr. N's classroom was the absolute farthest corner of the school. I had passed through three locked doors to reach it. A smiling, tall, thin man answered my knock and swept me in with a gesture of his long arms while telling students "sit down" and "be quiet." Kids were up and wandering, talking and calling out. A few students were working on a grammar lesson he had painstakingly written out on the chalkboard. The classroom looked like a transient apartment, nothing on the walls, no student work displayed, chairs facing front, separated, in straight rows.

Later, Mr. N explained his reluctance to accept coaching, admitting "I was afraid for you to see my classroom."

He needn't have been. I'd seen that classroom before. It was just like my classroom at the start of my teaching career.

Finally in the door, I found an excuse to stay and help with a library that needed organizing. From the library nook, I made mental notes on the classroom environment. We would need to work on procedures, rules, and consequences immediately. His needy students presented a host of behavior issues. And they needed to sit in groups.

After dismissal, we sat at student desks in the quiet classroom. I assured him that my role was to support and guide him — not to judge or evaluate. Relief washed over his face and he started to tell me about how he came to this "waiting place."

Turned out we were both career changers. His first teaching assignment started in that same classroom midway through the previous year in extremely trying circumstances. The former teacher, charismatic and beloved, also the popular choir director at a prominent South Side church, was found beaten to death in his apartment over Christmas break.

Mr. N walked into a class of angry, grieving, heartbroken kids. A situation that would try the ablest hands was entrusted to an untested new teacher. The kids resented him, as they would any replacement. I had seen students chew up three veteran teachers in an identical situation at my first school.

In urban communities where positive role models are scarce, schools are hungry for male teachers, especially men who reflect the cultural background of the student body. In that regard, Mr. N was a godsend. Not only was he a black man, he was an older black man. He had lived in Chicago all his life, graduated from city schools, worked as a city cop, and knew well the community around the school. He always walked me to my car after our meetings. He was intensely private. He had successfully dodged his coach his first partial year.

As late afternoon shadows wrapped around our conversation, I realized how brave Mr. N had been to come back for another year. He expressed determination to do better this year, his first full year.

As a new teacher, I had been roundly criticized for my failure to move thirty-six seventh-graders through the hallways in an orderly fashion. So I was particularly sensitive to the comments, sighs, and eye-rolling the school staff flagrantly directed toward Mr. N in that regard. Seeing their teacher's authority undermined, students responded by acting even worse. Teachers in the main building had an off-duty Chicago police officer stationed at the front desk all day as well as a disciplinarian within earshot of their voices. A steady stream of students filed to those two men all day, every day. There was no such backup in the mobile unit.

Mr. N's greatest behavior challenge was a boy who was barely reading, rarely turned in work, and was a bed wetter. Kids made fun of him because he often came to school smelling like urine. Mr. N spoke with the mother but nothing changed. So, unbeknownst to anyone else, Mr. N started taking home that child's laundry and returning it to him clean. That act of kindness, a quality in short supply in rough neighborhoods, convinced me that Mr. N

73

must succeed. He needed me because his students needed him, whether they knew it or not.

Effective teaching is about much more than caring and kindness, though. It was far more important for his students to progress as readers and Mr. N was struggling to implement balanced literacy. He attended workshops and monthly working meetings for beginning teachers while working on his science endorsement.

I felt confident that a "quick win" in classroom management would give him the time he needed for planning and instruction, and that student engagement would improve and encourage him. We broke down the line-up procedures and identified checkpoints, what to say, where to stand. We walked step-by-step through procedures: how to teach them, how to reinforce them, the need for consistency.

But the follow through fell through. His students continued to jostle in the hallways and bust loose as soon as they hit the outdoor area between the mobile unit and the school, with Mr. N running behind, scowling and demanding order. We continually discussed the imperative of effective management so that learning could take place. It was several months before Mr. N shared a success: he had started phoning students' homes and saw immediate improvement in behavior. I glanced at his classroom walls.

"Where are your rules?" I asked.

"Behind that other chart," he pointed.

I lifted the chart paper to expose the rules he had created the first week of school. There it was, number three under "Consequences": phone call home.

"There it was all along," he said, shaking his head at his lapse.

How did something as basic as classroom rules get pushed out of sight and out of mind? Clearly, Mr. N was overwhelmed. In the scramble to meet the many demands of a teacher's day, he was always harried. By his own admission, he was slow to master basic fundamentals of his practice because he constantly felt pulled in so many directions.

His principal chalked it up to personal weakness. She doubted his will.

"Do you think being isolated from the rest of the school is a factor?" I asked her.

"I never thought about that," she replied.

My second principal, an extraordinary leader, once told me, "Some teachers are born, some are made." She saw me as a born teacher because she did not see my first two years. I believe some teachers make themselves, through determination and commitment, serious study and reflection.

Why did I not see evidence of that same drive in Mr. N? Why was I spending time on the weekend painting green, yellow, and red on a "Stick of Justice" and putting students' names on twenty-two clothespins, only to see it, weeks later, gathering dust on his classroom windowsill? Where was the follow through?

Was I not hard enough on him? My role was not to judge or evaluate. But was support and guidance too soft? Should I have dressed him down like a student, like a child? As my first principal did to humiliate me? Mr. N was not me and I was not my abusive first principal. We were both adults and we urgently needed to step up to the challenges before us.

Analyzing student work revealed a wide range among Mr. N's learners, needs that would challenge even a seasoned teacher. He had a couple of nonreaders, one girl did not know her sight words. Vocabulary would be an important piece of their learning. Seeing that every student missed the same question on a reading test, we realized no one knew what a "flashback" was. Mr. N eventually did implement guided reading, which addressed the need for differentiation, but the challenge of managing and motivating the rest of the class while he was with groups was steep indeed.

With sixteen other new teachers on my coaching roster, I could not embed myself in Mr. N's classroom. And it was frustrating indeed when visits were canceled due to lost prep periods, schedule changes, and increasingly frequent testing. Three new tests were implemented to gauge whether students were on track for the big ISAT (Illinois Scholastic Aptitude Test) in the spring. Although these mandates infringed on our scarce time together, they also gave us data to analyze and plan from.

I got a fresh perspective on the schoolwide scramble for achievement when I arrived for a Monday morning visit and met the class walking into the gym, where they were to take yet another new test on laptops. They had been informed only minutes before. I went along to lend a hand and came away with a striking insight.

There were no procedures, no preparation, no plan for the testing day. Laptops were handed out, but students did not have the IDs and passwords they needed to log on. When that information was finally rounded up, many students had difficulty following the oral instructions.

The assistant principal and a security guard reprimanded students who were off-task and cast out four who would not behave. The others spent more than an hour trying to get on the computers and take the test. Although fourth- and fifth-graders were in the class, the test was for fifth-graders only. In the end, only four students were able to actually take the test. It was an epiphany: Mr. N's classroom was a microcosm of the school!

Was he doing the best anyone could under these circumstances? Certainly, I saw him making an effort to meet the many demands placed on him. But it seemed that expectations shifted with the wind; an impatient system desperate for quick results does not encourage habits of organization and consistency. A patient, steadfast mentor would be an important model. I could not lose faith.

"Do the Best You Can with the Time You Have," I embroidered on a sampler at Christmastime. It was evidence that I was forgiving myself, acknowledging my limitations. I saw that I had done the best I could my first

years as I continued to grow. I chose to see the best in Mr.
N. Enough people were doing the opposite.

Late in the year our work took a new focus as the
principal announced plans to make Mr. N the upper grade
science teacher the following year. In the end, the job
change did not occur. Mr. N started the next year back in
his bunker and on another coach's roster. When I heard he
was dodging that coach, I took him back onto my roster.

Just weeks later, the board of education announced it
was closing the school and the schoolwide panic that pre-
cedes annual standardized testing was overshadowed by a
campaign to keep the school open. In demanding higher
scores from Mr. N's students, the principal informed him
that there were four hundred teachers looking for jobs,
and if he couldn't do it, others were waiting for the
opportunity.

At the end of the year, the board of education reversed
its decision to close the school, acknowledging serious
safety concerns about students traveling farther to other
schools. Meanwhile, the district faced a budget crisis
of unprecedented proportions. Thousands of untenured
teachers were informed that their services were no longer
required. Mr. N was one of them. He was hurt but not
so discouraged that he bailed out of teaching, the choice
made by one in three new teachers by year three.

Our final meetings were spent reviewing sample
résumés and organizing his own. He was buoyed to see
his solid list of accomplishments and experiences. I had
been slow as a mentor to embrace and accept credit for
what I knew. Now I was encouraging him to do the

same. We spoke frankly about the challenges that had prevented him from being more successful in terms of student achievement, including whether I had provided appropriate and sufficient support to him as his coach.

"Are you kidding?" he said, surprised. "I would never have made it as far as I did without you. Now it's up to me to step up to the plate."

Those are words of determination, not defeat. His plans for the future revealed a perspective reaching far beyond his bunker and his school: he said he intended to work as a substitute to experience different grades and schools, with the goal of finding a setting where he can succeed. Effective school leadership, a supportive and inclusive environment, and the groundwork we laid together will help this new teacher find his place. In our time together, we both moved on from "the waiting place."

Reflective Questions

- Which mentoring tensions could you identify in this vignette?

- Which presented the greatest challenges for the mentor? Why?

- What factors contributed to the complexity of this coaching relationship?

- What evidence do you see of a trusting relationship?

- What evidence do you see of teacher growth?

- Who demonstrated leadership in this situation? How?

- Have you experienced similar situations? How did you negotiate the tensions?

- How were you able to influence the situation?

Fired, Hired, and Inspired

Mr. Z is teaching a ninth-grade science class when we first meet him. The mentor, whose own knowledge in science is wanting, sees right away that there are many things she can do that will help Mr. Z in his teaching. He has had no student teaching experience but loves science even when he is overwhelmed in his class. Building trust becomes the first task of the mentor. Although Mr. Z gets a negative evaluation, the mentor sees him as a teacher with real strengths and great possibilities. Mentoring Mr. Z calls on the mentor's persistence, intelligence, and support—and it helps get Mr. Z to the right place at the right time.

Fired, Hired, and Inspired

by Kathleen Aldred

*M*r. Z was a "late hire," as they are called in the district. He arrived two days after the official opening of school, important days when the professional development outlining district priorities and expectations was presented to all teachers. He also had the misfortune of not being invited to the New Teacher Institute that was held prior to the opening of school. Two weeks after school began, I was assigned to him: a name, a school, and an e-mail address on a slip of paper. I contacted him, asking if I could drop by the next day prior to his first class.

Getting in the Door

On Friday morning, after a twenty-minute search for a parking space, I climbed the steep, worn steps to his third floor classroom. Arriving at the same time as the students, I observed Mr. Z standing at the whiteboard, back to the classroom, furiously writing out the day's lesson. He was tall, a long ponytail curled down his back, and an abundant beard adorned the lower part of his face. It seemed incongruous considering the button-down shirt and necktie he sported. He appeared oblivious to the noise and chaos as thirty ninth-graders popcorned into the room. The scene resembled a rumble in the park rather than a science laboratory as students gathered in the back of the class, exchanging high-fives, joking, jostling, eating, and drinking. Most of the debris ended up on the floor. The language was rough, loud, and liberally peppered with spicy parts of speech. I knew I was going to be in trouble before this scene even unfolded. I hadn't thought about physics since barely passing it in college, so I didn't have a lot of background knowledge. I hoped that Mr. Z did.

I quietly introduced myself to Mr. Z, apologized for being late, and took a seat near his desk. A headache had already begun and I resisted an incredible urge to silently slide out the door, away from the pandemonium. Mr. Z finally turned to face the class. Several times, he asked his students to take their seats, his soft voice becoming a bit louder with each request. Finally, a very tall young man bellowed from the center of the crowd, "Everybody, shut the ____ up. Mr. Z is trying to talk."

Astonishingly, or maybe not, the students began to settle down and take their seats. It seemed that Tall Paul might possess potential leadership qualities. Fifteen minutes past bell time, Mr. Z introduced the topic and began to instruct students about lab procedures. He assigned students to various groups and requested that they move to the appropriate table. Nobody moved. The request was made again, which resulted in students reverting to earlier behavior, yelling out insults emphasized by those overused epithets: "I ain't ____ working with him." "I'm not ____ movin'." "Don't ____ tell me what to do." And so on. This dialogue apparently convinced Mr. Z to drop the group work idea. His face had that peculiar look of fear coupled with self-preservation. At that moment he resembled a battlefield soldier who had realized defeat. It was clear who ran the room, and it wasn't Mr. Z.

It was now thirty minutes into a sixty-five-minute class. Although the objective was written on the board, I did not remember it being referred to, nor did the students appear to be aware of any expectations. Glancing around I observed iPods plugged in, phone conversations, and texting galore. Most of the young males wore baseball caps, the colors signaling silent messages of group affiliation.

Where to Begin?

If Mr. Z thought he might be in "over his head," I knew I was. Where to begin when everything needed fixing? Classroom management was clearly at the top of the list; however, lesson planning was right alongside it. What about rules, routines, procedures, building relationships with the students? How do I start the conversation? Will he tell me he does not need a mentor? Does he see what I see? I felt like this classroom needed a team of EMTs (emergency mentor teachers) to descend on it and set up triage, with each team member focusing on one single area of support. I could not handle this alone. I scribbled notes on the students' behaviors and interactions, the teacher's movements and instructions, and drew a quick sketch of the room until space ran out on the data collection form. How long could this go on?

Establishing a Relationship

Mercifully, class ended. As students poured out of the room, Mr. Z told me his next block was free and we could talk. We reintroduced ourselves and sat down. I did not dare pull out the notes and instead asked him a few questions about himself (where he had received teacher training, where he completed student teaching, and so on). Mr. Z revealed that until the day he began teaching at this school, he was a cook and had pursued a degree in science part-time over several years. He had done a little substitute teaching in a couple of upper-class suburbs south of the city. I learned that he was a chef in a very upscale restaurant and still worked there on Saturday evenings. He had not taken an education program and had done no student teaching. He simply loved science and wanted to share this with others. He told me of a couple instances when he had formed a tentative relationship with a challenging student. Mr. Z was not oblivious to the situation, as I surmised, simply uninformed and overwhelmed. I explained the mentoring program and asked him to tell me two things he might like to improve in his classroom. I did not want him to be daunted by the fact that there were many things that needed improvement. He quickly stated, "I want them to sit down when they enter the room and I want them to stop swearing." We discussed how he wanted the students to enter the room, where he thought he should be, what message he was sending to his students if all they saw was his back when they came in, assigning a "do now," which he had never heard of, and having his lesson on the board before students came to class. He promised to work on procedures for beginning class over the weekend. The swearing, I would have to think about. As I walked through the school, it was apparent that foul language was an accepted part of the culture. We made an appointment for the following week. But I felt that I really couldn't help him because I felt so overwhelmed by his needs and he didn't even know what he needed. I secretly dreaded going back.

At home that night I thought about my morning in Mr. Z's classroom. Despite the data I had collected, two things brought me back to his class the next week. He loved science and he liked these kids. And I suspected that they liked him. I got to the classroom early and observed the new entry plan. Mr. Z positioned himself in the doorway, which meant students could only enter one at a time. He firmly grasped the hand of each student, shook it, and said, "Good morning, _____." Incredulously, I observed each student reply, "Good morning, Mr. Z." Each student then picked up a paper from a stack on the end of a table and sat down.

We had talked about starting with a warm-up activity (called the "do now" in our district). It is a five- to seven-minute activity that is a review of previously learned material. The purpose of it is for the students to get quickly into their seats, gain instant success at being able to complete it, and act as a starting point for the day's new learning. It took thirty-five minutes. During our debriefing, I praised his entry procedure. He confided that the secret was in not letting go of a student's hand until he or she greeted him back and confessed that the first few attempts did not go well, but after four days, they got it. Also, if a student had food or drink, he asked him or her to finish it in the hallway before entering the class. I pulled out the thirty-five-minute script on the do now. He read it and was astonished at the length of time it had taken.

By mid-October, things had settled a bit in room 308. Twice weekly observations and debriefs helped as well as lots of e-mail and phone communication. I harbored some guilt about spending so much time supporting Mr. Z. I had begun to view my caseload in a differentiated way:

from most needy to most independent. It was clear that Mr. Z needed extra support if his students were going to be successful. This was a departure from the past two years when I strove to give every teacher equal time, and I wrestled with this for the rest of the year. Gradually, we had begun to trust each other. For me, it meant that he would follow through with the next steps we decided on together. For him it meant that I would be a confidential sounding board who would always return for the next meeting.

Mr. Z appeared unfazed during the next few weeks. Because he had acquired some management skills and the class was not as chaotic, he was actually able to get through much of a lesson. Many students were keeping some sort of science notebook, but I knew this would not be enough to merit a satisfactory evaluation. He was due to be evaluated in two weeks.

I was worried for him. I knew that the headmaster was direct, to the point, and not very generous with praise. We discussed the district teaching standards for which he would be accountable and I suggested that we construct the lesson plan together. Mr. Z, however, did not appear to be worried. He assured me that he could do the lesson plan on his own and that his administrator "liked" him. I met with him before school started on the day of his evaluation. Mr. Z presented me with a thorough lesson plan that contained all of the required elements and he had a copy of it for his administrator. We rehearsed how things should go. He was pretty confident. He had been able to build relationships with several of the key players in each class and felt that these students would "have his back" when the administrator was in the classroom. I left with some encouraging words and went on to visit another classroom. He e-mailed me that evening stating that things had gone well.

A Negative Evaluation

Three days later, I received an upsetting e-mail from Mr. Z. He had just come from a meeting with his administrator where he was asked to sign off on his evaluation. It shocked him that his practice was described as "underperforming" in a number of areas. Most notably, lesson planning was cited, but also classroom management, professional behavior, assessment, and several others. He was devastated and told me that he would not be returning to the classroom after Thanksgiving. I wanted to call him immediately but did not know what to say. None of my other beginning teachers had quit. They had all returned to the classroom the following September. Failure had come to me for the first time in the middle of my third year as a mentor. Mr. Z and I had collaborated on the lesson plan. We planned, rehearsed, practiced. He had a copy of the evaluation document in advance and knew what the administrator was looking for. I felt that I had let him down and myself as well. If he left, it would be my fault. The administrator would lose respect for me and the NTC mentoring program, the students would be angry, and I would have to break in a new teacher midway through the school year. Almost immediately, I was ashamed of my thoughts. I had been thinking of how his departure would affect my reputation and my ability to do my job well. I had not considered how he felt. I knew that Mr. Z was planning to be married in April and that if he left this position, he would not be able to obtain another job in the system. I knew that he had relocated from the Midwest and had a temporary living situation. I knew he liked the kids and I thought he liked being a teacher. I decided not to call him and instead sent an e-mail stating that I would be in by 6:30 the following morning. We often met at this time of day because Mr. Z arrived to school around 6 AM and his first class began at 7:40. I still had no idea what I would say.

Wednesday morning, I arose early and forced myself to sit down and compile a list of all the reasons Mr. Z should not leave teaching:

- The kids really like you.
- You like the kids. You have a genuine affinity for them and understand their tough living circumstances.
- Students come at lunch and after school for tutoring and extra help.
- Classroom management is much better.
- You received an in-focus machine from DonorsChoose .com. (You have to use it!)
- You got a bunch of physics texts from DonorsChoose .com. Ditto.

- You spend as many as twelve hours a day at school. (This shows me you care.)

- You passed the MTELS.

- You're getting married in a few months. You need an income.

- The kids hardly swear anymore in your class.

Respect in the Classroom

The swearing had dissipated because of a strategic plan we devised and Mr. Z implemented. The issue had come up several times in September and October. Finally, I suggested that he set aside a class period in each block and just put the issue on the table. Initially, he did not want to do this, citing the pacing guide. Mr. Z was already behind and did not want to make things worse. I knew I had to push him on this and was frustrated that on the one hand he frequently mentioned how much it bothered him, yet on the other hand he was hesitant to confront the students and make it a non-negotiable. Just when I thought I was making some movement toward collaboration with Mr. Z, an issue such as this would arise and send me right back into instructive mode. Albeit reluctantly, I pointed out that he had to make a choice and the time was now. He had to decide either to live with it for the remainder of the school year or take action. We came up with a set of questions:

- Why do you swear?

- What is the impact on other people in the room?

- How does it make you feel?

- Is there another way you can express yourself without being offensive?

He did not teach any science the next day and turned the issue over to the students. I was not present that day. However, the next time I was in the room, I noticed a change. There was still swearing but a lot less of it and the students would immediately catch themselves with a quick, "Oh, sorry, Mr. Z."

On Wednesday morning, I arrived before school began, sat down, and presented Mr. Z with my list of reasons he should not quit. Some were pretty lame, but I asked him a question: "How do you think these kids are going to feel if they return after Thanksgiving and you are not here?" He admitted that he thought some would be angry and upset and that he thought they might feel that they had been abandoned, that he had given up on them. I told him that I thought a lot of adults had given up on them already and that might be why they were so mistrustful of him in the beginning of the year. I pointed out that he had worked very hard to build relationships with the kids. Did he want to dismiss all that hard work? Attendance was good. Few students cut his classes. They felt safe in his room. I asked him what he would do if he left teaching and he replied that he would go back to cooking full time. So he had a plan. This was not good.

I encouraged him to think seriously about the consequences of his decision and wished him a happy

Thanksgiving. I finished the morning, went home to prepare for my own Thanksgiving, and held my breath, waiting for Monday morning, and wondering if he would be in room 308 when his students returned from their own holiday.

Over the weekend, I sent a casual e-mail, asking how Thanksgiving went and wondering if we could meet Wednesday morning. No reply. Bad omen. To my surprise, Tuesday evening, I received an e-mail, with the familiar greeting "Hiya, Kathleen." In it, he thanked me for putting up with him and agreed to meet. I realized that he was straddling the fence between survival and disillusionment. I let out a long sigh of relief, feeling that I had been holding my breath for a week.

Mr. Z was in a decidedly better frame of mind the next morning. I thought the break had been good for both of us. However, so sure was I that he would indeed quit, I had no plan in place for next steps. For now, he was the teacher of record, but for how long and how could I sustain his interest and desire to continue teaching in this incredibly unsupportive environment? I would have to follow his lead. Meanwhile, I had realized that the administrator had been avoiding meeting with me for a while, despite several requests. I wondered about this and attributed it to his busy schedule. I also felt that if he had serious concerns about Mr. Z's practice, he would have spoken to me.

We forged a plan to get him through until the winter holidays, which were three weeks away. He was still down a lot, still mentioning going back to cooking full time, but we began to focus on lesson planning and eventually graduated from day-to-day lessons to attempting a full week at a time. This gave Mr. Z a focus other than the behaviors of the students. I was in Mr. Z's classroom twice a week and noticed that things went more smoothly when he stuck to the lesson plan. Some kids took notes, some didn't, but when he incorporated experiments into the plan, student engagement was definitely higher. I thought that this could be a key component in his planning. We talked about it and he pointed out his lack of materials and classroom supplies and explained that in order to conduct an experiment, he would have to round everything up from various sources and usually had considerable out-of-pocket expenses. I had to back off on the experiments for the time being. Mr. Z made it through to the beginning of the holiday season. We had twelve days off and I urged him not to think about school too much and to relax and have fun.

Winter Break: Creative Juices Flowing

Mr. Z was the first teacher I visited at the conclusion of the winter break. The time off was definitely beneficial. He seemed more relaxed and his sense of humor was returning. He talked very excitedly about two projects he wanted to implement. One of his ideas was an MCAS (Massachusetts Comprehensive Assessment System) preparation class that he would conduct after school

Monday through Thursday. The other was on Fridays he would teach a film animation class. It sounded like burnout to me because this was a teacher who had already taken six sick days since September. I suggested that he start gently with the MCAS prep class, perhaps one or two days, so that the "students" would not burn out. The prep class was reduced to just Tuesdays in the beginning. At first, five or six students showed up, but by May, he had fifteen or sixteen students coming by and had expanded the session to two days a week. The film animation class on Fridays was immensely popular with both students and teachers. Twenty or so people stayed after school every Friday. These two initiatives seemed to validate Mr. Z's efforts to be effective in his school. The day-to-day classroom routines had improved slightly but he still needed support. He had started giving weekly quizzes and I noticed that on quiz day, usually Friday, absenteeism was high. There was no procedure in place for making up the quiz, so assessment was uneven, at best. Generally, he graded students based on an average of their quiz marks and their behavior. Too many students were failing. I suggested rethinking the weekly quizzes as the only solid assessment of student work and we tried to brainstorm some formative assessments instead. I reminded him of the daily summaries he asked the students to complete. Many times this was a rushed attempt at the end of class and was done poorly, if at all. We made a plan that for a solid week he would insist that every student complete the daily summary (ticket to leave) and that he would date stamp them, collect and grade them, and return them to the students in a timely manner. His response was that it seemed like a lot of work, but he would try it. At the same time, I mentioned the binders that (some) students took notes in. Although required by the district, this, again, was lopsided. Some students kept perfect binders, sectioned off, complete notes, and so on, which were never looked at by the teacher. Other students made half-hearted attempts to keep a binder, and many students didn't even bother to bring one to class. A new term was about to begin, so I asked him to think about making the binders a meaningful tool for the students. His plan could commence with the beginning of the new term. Mr. Z decided to collect and grade the binders every two weeks, as other teachers in the school were doing. The binders would represent 20 percent of the students' grade. It would be a huge amount of work and I knew it wouldn't last if the task were too overwhelming. As the first deadline neared, Mr. Z reminded his students daily that he would be collecting binders on Friday. He had adopted a rubric from another teacher and would use this to assess the binders. He decided to give the students an independent assignment and assess as many binders as possible during class. When I checked in the following week, Mr. Z informed me that about 75 percent of the students turned in a binder, that he was able to look at only half of them during school time, including his planning time and lunch, and that he remained in school until 6 PM Friday evening, assessing binders after the film animation class had concluded. But he was pretty happy with the effort because the contents of the binders overall were pretty good. He felt that they would take less time to assess as he got better at it and decided to permanently adopt this effort.

Getting Fired and Getting Married

Some time in February, Mr. Z received a blow. He was informed by his administrator that he would not be getting a reasonable assurance letter, which would have ensured him of a position the following September, and that his job would be posted. He was encouraged by the administrator to reapply for the position and he took this to mean there was hope that he could return to the school. I knew, however, that in the district, this was a polite way of saying "you're fired" but could not tell Mr. Z that. I encouraged him to apply for his own job as well as any other science position the district had posted. He submitted an application for his position and waited patiently to be summoned for an interview. It never happened and his mood sunk lower and lower. I felt like it was September all over again as far as my support went. I could never give him enough encouragement. He tried to put on a good face in the classroom and did not want the students to find out that he wouldn't be back. It was a tough act and he went home feeling defeated daily. As Mr. Z's mid-April wedding drew closer, he decided to chalk up this year as "an experience I will never forget" and to go back to the restaurant business full time when the school year was over.

I felt even worse than he did. I had never mentored a more hard-working, sincere, and caring individual. In speaking with other teachers in the building, I discovered that the principal had already hired his replacement and never had any intention of interviewing Mr. Z again. In fact his replacement was an adorable twenty-something female who was the student teacher intern in the class next door and had been promised the position in October! It seemed like every teacher in the school knew this except Mr. Z. His wedding coincided with spring break and I decided to hold off on this information for as long as possible.

Teaching in an Alternative School

In the meanwhile, across town at an alternative high school where I mentored four teachers, I learned that there would be a science position open for the following school year because one of my beginning teachers was relocating to Denver. Although the faculty was pretty relaxed and informal at this school, I wondered if they would seriously consider Mr. Z for the position. Even here, he would be noticed. I also wondered if Mr. Z would even consider applying for the position after the way he had been burned at the other school. This school was conducting a symposium of student work on an evening in May. The public was invited and it took every persuasive skill I possessed to convince Mr. Z to accompany me to the symposium. I conveyed to him that, although he had had a poor experience in his school, there were many great schools in the district where his skills would be appreciated and that this was one of them. I begged him to take a look, that he had nothing to lose.

On that tenuous night in May, Mr. Z fell in love with the school. He spoke with faculty, students, and parents and felt comfortable and at home with the unusual curriculum and atmosphere. But again, self-doubt arose. "Why would they even consider me when there are so many experienced science teachers out there?" he asked. By now, he knew about the duplicity of his administrator and would not ask him for a job recommendation. Two other teachers at his school and a science department coach he had been working with were willing to give him recommendations, so he applied for the position. I was aware that the alternative school had already interviewed several candidates and wanted to make a decision soon, so I approached the science department head at the school and made a strong case for waiting a while longer and granting an interview to Mr. Z.

The school invited Mr. Z to an interview and lesson presentation two days later. His lesson (making electricity from lemons) blew them away! The students were captivated, as was the interview panel (four science teachers and the head of the school). He was offered the job by the end of the day. I could have wept with relief. His long, difficult journey into the world of teaching was not in vain.

Three years later, Mr. Z continues to enlighten his students about the mysteries of science at the alternative school. This past year, he was awarded a $40,000 grant to transform his classroom into a physics lab. It is a delightful place. He's made it a green classroom, eco-friendly, state of the art, and a magnet for students. The self-doubt about his teaching skills has vanished. Mr. Z continues to improve his craft, but most of all he is still a teacher, having achieved tenure in the district this past September. His former administrator, however, was removed from his position at the end of Mr. Z's first year and is no longer employed by the district.

Reflective Questions

- What might Mr. Z not have known about teaching when he began this assignment?

- What elements may have contributed to the relationship between the mentor and the beginning teacher?

- What role did the administrator play in the teacher's early failures in the classroom?

- What could the mentor have done differently to avoid some of the cliff-hanging incidents in this story?

- At an early point (before his evaluation) Mr. Z thinks he is doing a good job and that he will get a positive evaluation. What factors may have contributed to this sense of euphoria?

- To what degree do you think Mr. Z's administrator should have extended extra time to him?

- Could Mr. Z's mentor have been more proactive around incorporating experiments into the daily lesson?

- What factors may have helped this beginning teacher gain tenure in the district?

STORY THREE
Finding a Way

In a remote town in Alaska, we find a mentor trying to figure out how to establish a relationship with her mentee. The mentee, Angela, is in her second year of teaching, initially from the Midwest. The mentor is greeted by Angela's comment that she doesn't need a mentor this year. In struggling to find a place to start, the mentor connects to her mentee by suggesting that their focus could be on the students in the high school basic English class. Swallowing her own discomfort in dealing with teenagers (not her area of expertise) and resisting the urge to dive in with suggestions, we follow the slow build up of a focus on students and a way of working strategically with Angela. Two steps forward and one step backward, the mentor finds her way.

Finding a Way

by Mary Eldred

We didn't get off to a great start. Angela was added to my list of early career teachers three weeks into the school year. My first opportunity to meet Angela was late September. As I flew over the magnificent Alaska Range and then over thousands of acres of small lakes, swamps, and flat tundra to her remote town in southwest Alaska, the feeling of isolation prevailed. I could only imagine what she, a young college graduate from the Midwest, thought as she flew into her new home and first teaching job a year ago. I was anxious to meet her. I wanted to start mentoring immediately. But that was not to happen. I was to learn some integral lessons about mentoring through my work with Angela. It's truly not about what I want, and it's not even about what the teacher wants; the students are the reason we mentor. How do we maintain the level of trust with our teachers so that we can get to the heart of the issues and when we do, how do we know if we are being effective?

Establishing a Relationship: Getting in the Door

"I really don't need a mentor this year. It's my second year, I'll be fine without a mentor. I know what I'm doing now," Angela remarked when we met during her lunchtime. She was already well into her plans for her classes, teaching literature to high school students for the second year, and she felt she had a good handle on what was necessary to be an effective teacher. How was I to convince her that I could be an asset?

Building Trust

As much as I wanted to, I did not visit her classroom that first day. Without the element of trust, an observation could be intimidating. I decided to meet her after school and have dinner together. We talked about personal things: family, friends, and interests and how she was coping with the isolation. Although this Alaskan town was not as remote as some of the ones I visit, there are no roads in or out, only two grocery stores, and little in the way of social opportunities. In our conversation Angela mentioned her concerns with her basic English classes, groups of students that, for some reason or another, were not ready for a standard high school English class. We agreed to focus our work on those remedial classes. Instead of putting the spotlight on Angela and her teaching, and thus risking defensiveness, the focal point of our work was the students. They needed support, a purpose for learning, and the skills and strategies to be successful readers and writers.

Can I Really Help?

Teenagers frighten me. I was not entirely comfortable in the high school setting. My twenty years of teaching were in elementary classrooms, where students still love their teachers, hugs are abundant, and a stern look is enough to keep students in line. My years of mentoring experiences have tempered my insecurities about working in a high school, but sometimes I still feel like an outsider.

On my initial visit to Angela's basic English class, I looked around at the students: a group of girls sat together whispering and giggling; a group of boys up front quietly worked; a few other boys on the perimeter, sullen, disinterested, hoods up, heads down on their desks; a girl in front of me put her head down and went to sleep. "How would I handle this kind of apathy if I were the teacher here?" I wondered to myself. Angela was enthusiastic and animated. The topic was parts of speech. "What is a noun? What is a verb?" Angela asked walking around the room, appealing for responses. The boys in front answered in single words. Angela did most of the talking. Next, books were passed out. *Earthquake!* was the title. Angela had struggled to find literature on a lower reading level that would be interesting to a group of teenagers. This was one of the few titles she found in the school for which there were multiple copies and could possibly hold their interest. Students read quite fluently when they were called on, but attempts at discussions were fragmented. Questions collided with silence. Angela ended the fifty-minute period with an audible sigh but was smiling again before the students in the next period, another basic English class, sauntered in. Watching Angela teach, I could see such potential. The threads of effective teaching were there. I saw her desire to be the best teacher she could possibly be. How could I, a former elementary teacher, guide her in teaching these at-risk teenagers?

Small Steps

I wanted Angela to trust me and find value in our work together. I so much wanted to dive in. I wanted to talk about engagement strategies; things to do before, during, and after reading; using assessments to guide instruction, and so on but I knew I needed to hold back. I didn't want her to get defensive about her teaching. I reminded myself to keep the focus on the students and the data I had obtained in my observation.

During our debriefing, we talked about her strengths: good rapport with students, organized, enthusiastic, plenty of teacher scaffolding. We discussed the lack of motivation of many of the students, their resignation to failure, and what she could do to convince them that education was important. It really did seem futile. I reminded myself to listen and to ask questions. I asked, "What do you know for sure about their reading abilities?" Although they seemed to be fluent readers, she wasn't sure if they were understanding what they read. Here was my entry point. It was decided that we'd start with a comprehensive reading assessment to pinpoint the students' reading strengths and weaknesses.

Finding Direction: Collecting Data

For my next visit I came in during lunch. Rather than being in the teachers' lounge visiting with other teachers, Angela was in her classroom. Students were scattered around the room: playing chess, using laptops, working on assignments. Angela was conferring with two students at her desk, encouraging them to get late work turned in for other teachers, making them to-do lists. She oozed energy. Students did not want to leave at the end of the lunch period. She shooed them out with a smile. Barely taking a breath, she started the first basic English class of the day. Half-sheets of paper were passed out...top part, write about your favorite holiday; bottom part, give examples of three nouns, three proper nouns, three action verbs. The room was quiet, some students wrote, others left the paper blank. I was introduced as a mentor, a teaching partner, and that we would be doing a reading assessment with each student. Again, I was impressed that most students read quite fluently but when it came to retelling, the teenagers became silent. "My brain doesn't hold that stuff," one of them replied. Most could not tell me the setting, characters, or plot of the one-page stories they had just read to me.

Angela and I met after class to look at the results. "But I taught them what a setting was!" she lamented. "Does this mean they might not remember the plot of the book we've been reading for two weeks?" "Probably not," I thought to myself. It was again time to ask questions. "What strategies are you using to help them comprehend? What have you done to build their background knowledge? How are they able to understand the vocabulary?" I wrote furiously while she talked. Then ideas began flowing: differentiating, story boards, vocabulary lessons, and so on. Suddenly, we really were teaching partners with a common goal. By listening, using my mentoring questioning strategies, and focusing on students, our work together had taken a sense of direction. We were talking about teaching strategies in the context of how it would affect the students, and I finally felt we were on our way to an effective mentoring relationship. But how could I be sure?

As a classroom teacher, I usually knew when I was being effective. I could look at student work and see improvement. I had pretests and posttests as well as feedback from students, parents, and administrators, but as a mentor, how do I know if I am being effective? My first step is to develop trust, to develop a relationship so the teacher is comfortable sharing, venting, and exposing inadequacies, perceived or real. We listen, observe, take data, provide feedback, and offer suggestions. Is it my presence, the data, and my suggestions that move teachers' practices forward, or is it the process of reflecting on their own teaching, knowing their students, the curriculum, and the community as well as their own desire to be the best they can be?

Angela seemed to feel the same urgency. By January, she was already thinking of next year and ways to improve her instruction. I was thrilled that she had already decided to stay and continue teaching, but there was still a need to plan for the current school year. "What do your basic English students need to know by the end of the year?" State tests were looming and she could feel the pressure. Our attention was redirected to the present year and we spent time creating a plan, identifying the skills students needed and how she was going to accomplish teaching those skills. Nouns, verbs, and pronouns became part of students' writings. Isolated writings became part of a journal to monitor progress. Angela was now able to explain to students the why, or the purpose, of their studies.

Losing Footing

Teaching a full load of literature classes as well as the two periods of basic English classes that few teachers wanted, coaching girls' basketball as well as the debate team, helping with theatrical performances, and taking college classes, Angela was a busy woman. On one of my spring visits, I observed in her class and took notes on things I noticed and things I had questions about. I usually found this method of taking data an effective way to frame a follow-up conversation. Due to Angela's prior commitments, we were not able to debrief. I left my notes in her mailbox, planning on going over them during a weekend phone call. The following day I received an e-mail from Angela defending each point I had raised in my observation. In one swoop, I had put her on the defensive. I had learned another valuable lesson. Although my work with her was nonevaluative, it could be perceived as critical. Balanced with conversation, it is a way to move forward, but without the personal conversation it can be viewed as a one-sided attack. Would I be able to regain her trust again? Once again I needed to step back and focus the attention on the students.

Angela was a master at supporting her students. She modeled her expectations, divided lessons into small steps, and planned group projects. She wanted to take these students who were so familiar with failure to a place where they could feel successful. Yet, she was hesitant in pushing them toward independence. When we sat down and looked at the state test scores it became evident that it was time to increase the expectations. It was time to get serious. The writing scores were glaringly low.

There were opportunities for students to write in her class: journal writing, sentences to expand, summaries of stories they've read. "How are you assessing what they write and tailoring your instruction to their needs?" I asked. "I'm just glad when they write," Angela replied. Here was my chance to use the analyzing student work (ASW) tool.

We began planning on Monday for my Friday visit. I asked for a set of student writing samples so that we could do an ASW. "We're working on summaries of the book we're reading in class. I've guided them in summary writing; should I bring those?" she wrote in an e-mail. "Perhaps something that has less of your input," I replied. "Journals, then?" "Aren't those meant as a means of communication between you and your students? It really wouldn't be fair to use them to assess their writing skills." She decided she would give the class a prompt "If I Were One Inch Tall" and a time limit. I was looking forward to the opportunity to really analyze the students' writing needs and help Angela plan her writing instruction to meet those needs.

Dealing with Trauma

The instant I walked into the building on Friday afternoon, I could sense tension. An unnatural stillness replaced the usual hum of the commons area. Students milled around, some sat on the benches, but there was not the teenage energy and the usual animated, boisterous conversations I encountered on previous visits. A student had attempted suicide at the school. Shock, questioning, and feelings of helplessness permeated the air in hushed conversations. Surely I couldn't ask Angela to focus on assessing students' writing after this. But she insisted we do just that. "What a testament to her dedication as a teacher," I thought to myself. "Not only was it a Friday evening, it was a Friday evening after a very traumatic day."

117

I braced myself to find fragments of writing, undeveloped sentences and ideas, but we were pleasantly surprised. Stories in the Yupik culture tell of a little people who live among them, sometimes creating mischief, so the topic was familiar. It was obvious that many of the students had enjoyed the assignment and were very creative in their ideas. We were able to sort the papers into groups, identify needs, and move to instructional steps. Angela was able to move through the process almost instinctively and was delighted to figure out her next steps in teaching writing for each group.

A week later I received an e-mail: "Their writing is so much better! We've been working on revising. I think they're getting it. I think I get it!"

Arriving

In a mentor's life, this was better than an award, better than a raise. Angela was differentiating for students' needs, building on their strengths, working with their weaknesses, and seeing the results. By focusing on the students, we developed a road map for our work. The common destination built camaraderie and trust and I reveled in the shadow of her success.

Reflective Questions

- How important is trust in a professional relationship?

- How can the effectiveness of mentoring be gauged?

- In what ways was the mentor effective?

- What tools might the mentor use to keep the focus on students rather than the teacher?

- When a postconference is not possible, what are some ways the mentor might share data without making the teacher defensive?

- What is our role as mentors in traumatic situations? How do we best function as a support?

- In the face of opposition to being mentored, what might be a mentor's best approach or position?

·STORY ONE·
The Waiting Place

·STORY TWO·
Fired, Hired, and Inspired

·STORY THREE·
Finding a Way

STORY FOUR
Savior, Friend, Mentor

Savior, Friend, Mentor

The mentor tries to help his mentee fight his often-felt frustration in dealing unsuccessfully with students and blaming them for classroom failures. The mentor tries to rise above the chaos by attempting to overcome the lack of supplies and lack of student motivation and deal with a school that is dysfunctional in many ways. In his frustration, the mentor realizes he must show, not tell, and he does this by engaging his mentee in experiences where he can learn and gain insights into his students. Through their developing friendship, the mentor realizes that he must understand his own struggles with his mentee's argumentative nature and focus on using the skills and abilities he has to effectively mentor his mentee, in this case, focusing on pedagogy and strategies of classroom management. Trying to be savior and friend provides the mentor with the glue that eventually sticks, deepens the relationship, and helps the mentee to learn how to teach.

Savior, Friend, Mentor

by Frank Pantano

I n my efforts to mentor Marco effectively, a friendship grew, and out of that friendship boundaries were crossed, philosophical dilemmas emerged, and the multiple roles of a mentor shifted.

My subconscious mind must have realized how inexperienced and unprepared for teaching Marco was because my "savior" instincts were reawakened. Although I knew I was treading on dangerous ground, similar to the proverbial moth, I danced dangerously close to the flame. I not only attempted to interpret for Marco the intricacies of urban education, but in doing so also unhinged my own realities of mentoring by inviting him into my home to meet my friends and into my life.

At the August New Teacher Institute, I worked my way around the Eastern USA High School table introducing myself to my new group of beginning teachers. Marco introduced himself and in Spanish, I made my introduction, "Es un placer conocerte."

"The pleasure is mine," he replied "¿De donde eres and porque hablas el Español?"

"I am American, but bilingual. I majored in Spanish and Italian, lived in Spain, and taught school in Puerto Rico," I proudly replied in unaccented Español.

Thus the stage was set for my bilingual mentoring experience. Instantly, we hit it off. Marco's winning smile and the naïveté of a novice teacher were the hooks that led me to believe it would be an "easy challenge" to mentor this thirty-something Cuban exile—a career changer whose only experience in education had been four years as an adjunct Spanish professor at one of Boston's prestigious Ivy League colleges.

Teacher and Facilitator

For Marco the first days of school were an eye-opener. "What should I know about the Eastern USA High School?" Marco asked. "It is the oldest public high school in the United States and as a result of years of underperformance has been designated one of two Boston turnaround schools," I said. Under President Obama's school reform plan, with increased funding, administrative autonomy, and 190 hours of additional professional development, the school should get on track. Marco was one of an influx of new faculty members intended to effect this change.

In early September, Marco and I scanned the class rosters. He concluded, "This is a hodgepodge of special needs students, native Spanish speakers, and recent immigrants." He questioned, "Why do they have to take Spanish?" Armed with only his Massachusetts Test for Educator License in Spanish, Marco was lost, and even as an experienced teacher and mentor, I struggled with concrete solutions to offer that would be educationally sound and alleviate his anxieties.

On my first visit, I walked into a windowless classroom. One-third of it was filled with the previous teachers' accumulated years of materials: a mountain of boxes, exploding with old worksheets precariously piled to the ceiling, jury-rigged storage cabinets whose locks had been long ago smashed, and like the elephant in the room, a big black *piano*, a temptation for any mischievous adolescent!

Facilitator and Leader

I knew at this point that my mentoring work had only just begun. As a mentor, there are those who view me as someone with power, such as they would with a retired principal. So when I asked to have the mess in Marco's room removed I was quickly given access to an empty storage room, carts, and a few strong young men to begin the move. I soon experienced the extent of that power, however; one year later Marco was still waiting for his textbook order and his own LCD projector.

Routines and Procedures

To create community and cohesiveness in his classroom, one of our first steps was to institute some procedures and routines. "Marco, let's work on a consistent classroom arrangement, a seating plan, student folders, and an individual behavior chart with daily points," I suggested.

The Lesson Plan

"What is involved in a lesson plan? Is it really necessary to put the objectives on the board? How do they help the students to learn?" Marco asked with a puzzled expression.

"The content objectives frame what you want the students to be able to do at the end of the lesson; they help students to focus. They will also help to keep you on track," I explained.

The Behavior Plan

"But they talk too much and don't listen. So I just keep teaching and talk over them. I do not want to yell. Sometimes I do not even understand what they are saying. My English is not that good," he confessed.

"If they are talking, you should stop talking and do not try to talk over them. Remember to use the daily behavior and self-assessment rubric to collect data and help students to monitor their own behavior in class. Keep the students involved by speaking Spanish to them, miming your directions, and having them constantly repeat what you say."

Most days, Marco was tense, which, therefore, influenced my approach.

The Honeymoon

During these first few months of "honeymooning," Marco thanked me every day for "saving him." He was exhausted and told me that if were not for my presence he would have quit after a week. That was enough for me to persevere. His success with Ivy League students did not remotely prepare him for what he was to encounter at Eastern USA High, the polar opposite of the educational spectrum. Marco early on confessed to me that he had no formal pedagogical training and was equipped with only the METL (Massachusetts Test for Educator Licensure). Early on, I set up a cross-site visit. I want him to see other Spanish teachers in action.

Unimpressed, Marco and I watched students use PowerPoint presentations to describe life in Latin American countries in one native Spanish speakers' class. In Spanish I class, enthusiastic students entered to cheerful greetings of "Hola. ¿Como estas hoy? ¿Que dia es?"

Pointing to anchor charts and a word wall, the teacher encouraged even the most self-conscious of learners to attempt speaking rudimentary Spanish. This was exactly what I wanted Marco to emulate. "How can I get a job in a school like this? The students here are different than those at Eastern USA High," he said.

I was more interested in what Marco had gleaned from the experience because my role is to help build a more stable teaching force rather than provide a job placement service.

"But, Marco, what was the learning from today?" I pressed on. Marco acknowledged the need for more anchor charts, a more active presence in the classroom, but was still worried about his level of English proficiency.

"Mira, Marco, hablas muy bien el ingles, and the students understand you perfectly well. The key is to become more relaxed and comfortable while becoming more animated in your delivery," I counseled. "What do you think of me videotaping our next session? We can review it together to observe classroom behaviors that detract from student learning, your response, and teaching style. It will also be useful in helping assess the effectiveness of the daily behavior logs that you meticulously keep."

Marco's frustrations with classroom management mired his progress with instruction. The more he expressed his frustration with the Boston Public Schools, Eastern USA High School, and "these students'" lack of skills or even a fundamental desire to learn, the more I tried to listen, to defend, to make suggestions, and to find resources. I especially tried to explain to Marco the circumstances surrounding many of the students: poverty, racism, disenfranchisement, and the ills of urban education.

Weary of telling, I decided to show. One December weekend we went to see the movie *Precious*. As he sobbed, I suggested that from now on when questioning the apathy and anger of many of his students, he should reflect on his experience watching the movie. I explained that Precious could be any one of the angry, apathetic, volatile, and disengaged students in his classroom.

Christmas vacation was on the horizon. I realized that we were both in that new teacher trough of disillusionment. I was spending an inordinate amount of time in his classroom, on the phone, and at dinner meetings, simply supporting him to break the isolation of the classroom. I blurred the line between personal and professional lives. I questioned my professional instincts. Marco was becoming a friend.

However, he was avoiding the issues that needed to be addressed. In preparation for each visit I would think, "Will today be the right time to debrief the video, to complete a final response to his November 15 teacher evaluation, and review special education requests?"

Accelerating Teacher Development

My responsibility was to address these important issues; I only had one year to mentor him.

"I am afraid to tell you this, but today I had an excellent day in *all* of my classes," he greets me tentatively.

"That's great. Tell me why you think it was a great day and what you did that made the difference," I held my breath.

"Nine students were not in class today; the class was calm and excellent without 'those trouble makers,'" he explained.

"Great, but do you know where they were?" I asked. "You might want to check the attendance list to see if they were all absent," I suggested. I gulped, knowing this was not going to be a friendly conversation. Overwhelmed, frustrated, and exhausted, the safety valve of professional comportment was about to blow.

"Now you give me one more thing to do. No one has ever told me to do that. There is no system in the school and no accountability," he shouted.

One, two, three, I counted under my breath. "You should at least cover yourself because the headmaster holds you accountable for all of the students in the class, whether you want them there or not."

"How can I do this?" he barked, with fire in his eyes.

"A simple e-mail: 'the following students were not in my class today and were not marked absent on the master list,'" I calmly suggested.

"*No,* I will not add one more thing to my list of duties. It is not my role or responsibility and no one told me what to do," he countered.

I responded, "At the end of the term, when more than half the class fails, you will be asked what you did to help those students learn." My heart sank because I know that although students can be difficult and disrespectful, by not addressing the issue the message becomes, "I really don't want you there in the first place, so don't bother coming."

I could see the fire in his eyes as he began to yell louder, about the school needing a computerized system, and it being everyone else's responsibility, and that is when I stopped listening. Startled at his outburst, I loudly responded, "Don't raise your voice with me; there is no need to do that."

As he continued to rant, I picked up my briefcase and computer and told him I would meet him at the door to take him to an appointment that he had previously scheduled. "Don't bother," he snapped. "I'll take the bus." I met him in the lobby, knowing that I needed to rectify the situation.

In silence we drove to and from the appointment. "Why am I investing so much in him?" I questioned myself. Just as Marco can't choose his students, I can't choose mentees; just as all students deserve the very best you can give them, even if they don't want it, Marco deserves the best I can give him, even if it means I will not let him enjoy the "few good days that he has" when it is at the expense of another student's learning. Guilty, I was reminded when I too have felt relief when certain students were absent. Guilt is a powerful emotion for the "savior."

The Philosophical Dilemma of a Mentor

Too often, I am caught defending the system and the students to whom I have dedicated the past thirty-four years. My fear is that possibly I too have become numb to the dysfunction of urban education. Am I in collusion with a bankrupt system of education that fails students by not addressing their plethora of educational needs?

Realizing the limits of one person against the school system, I tried to refocus on Marco's personal professional goals. His major goal was to become more confident and skillful in classroom management. In the end, Marco was convinced that the only change needed were the students or at the very least, the Boston Public School policies. He was in serious denial.

The next two months were a cooling-off period. Marco treated mentoring respectfully but as a requirement. I, however, viewed it as an integral part of his personal growth and professional development but focused on his professional life. I wondered, does Marco really want to be a high school Spanish teacher? Although first-year Spanish may not be his forte, he is a natural in Spanish III and would excel in AP Spanish. How could I help get him into a situation that better suited his abilities?

A Different Perspective

A small group of teachers from Eastern USA High, including Marco and myself, enrolled in Critical Friends Group Training. As Critical Friends we would be versed in a number of protocols designed to deepen awareness and reflection and gain insight into our own educational practice. My intention in taking the course with Marco was for him to see that the reflective practice I was trying to instill in our relationship was also shared by a number of faculty members.

During this session, Marco was animated and with pride explained the relationships he had built with the students. He highlighted their progress: his first term 85 percent of the students failed, but the second term only 50 percent failed. This was an improvement but I wanted to ask him how we could get the other 50 percent to pass. What strategies could he use to decrease this dismal statistic, which only reinforces the notion that urban schools fail urban youth?

Marco beamed when analyzing big-picture problems. He was knowledgeable in his subject matter, and in Spanish-speaking classes he was certainly in control. His secondary goal was to let go so that the class would become more student centered.

With the spring thaw, we were able to get back on track. As I reflected on my own behavior, I realized that we both had grown. I realized that his intense argumentative nature had little to do with me. I also came to the realization that I often mistake intensity for anger, which I avoid at all costs. As a result conversations became easier. Marco was able to focus on the students and his craft as a teacher. The students who wanted to succeed began to come after school for extra help. A few who struggled also began to buckle down when they realized that the end of the year was approaching and in order to pass they needed to put more effort into their work.

There was also more turmoil; Eastern USA High was again named one of the most underperforming schools in the district. Under the restructuring plan, the headmaster was given the authority to remove up to 50 percent of the staff, and there was the threat that everyone would have to reapply. Simultaneously fearing unemployment and feeling the momentum of the upswing of rejuvenation, Marco was one of the fortunate ones. Reality had set in. Although Marco made waves and complained about the lack of continuity in the foreign language program and the total disregard for sequence-of-course studies in the school, he understood: the students deserved better, a higher standard and benchmarks to measure progress.

In June, as graduation approached, Marco was again in knots. He was asked to pass senior students who had never come to class or who had failed three out of four terms. The guidance counselors were trying to cover up mismanagement.

Every year, in celebration of a successful first year of teaching, I host a sit-down dinner at my home for my fifteen novice teachers. Marco toasted, stating that he would have quit in the first week if it were not for me. He acknowledged butting heads and reiterated that it was never about me personally but rather about the inequities in the school system.

Graduation day, June 17, 2010, was Marco's first. During the ceremony, one failed student angrily approached. "I'm gonna _____ you up; it's your fault that I did not graduate," he threatened.

Later that evening Marco called me in California. I was there attending a three-day workshop given by the New Teacher Center. Although my work with him had officially ended, I made myself available. I advised him to write up the incident, copying it to all of the administrators and school police. There was an official disciplinary hearing for the student, which resulted in only a two-day suspension.

Over the summer break, Marco and I had many opportunities to discuss his second year. He was eager to begin planning, especially for AP Spanish Language and also, he hoped, for Spanish III. As the summer waned, so did Marco's patience, his sense of renewal gave way to frustration in waiting for final course assignments. One week before school and he still had no word on course assignments.

"I will quit if they give me any Spanish I classes," he stated one day as I tried to reassure him that "this is how the system works. It sucks, but in my experience, schedules have never been finalized until the day before school starts, and sometimes not even then." I began to question why and how we could change this system of uncertainty.

Another year, few textbooks to be found, no LCD projector, but a new room with windows and a renewed spirit. Routines and procedures were in order and reinforced daily. The word wall was up, the student work folders made, and some initial formative assessments prepared.

Marco still complains about the system but in his resolve to teach he has toughened up. He calls parents regularly before incidents happen. He has a proven routine and well-balanced lessons.

On September 14, 2010, I sat proudly among more than five thousand excited foreigners anxiously assembled with their guests in historic Fenway Park. With tears of pride and joy streaming down our faces, I witnessed Marco's swearing in as a U.S. citizen. This was a momentous day for both of us, symbolizing freedom, friendship, and a commitment to the ideals of the United States. As mentors, our work crosses personal and professional boundaries. It can present difficulties. It also can positively affect the work and move it forward. One of the official speakers at the ceremony urged these new citizens to take an active part by exercising their new political power. I urged Marco to use his in making a better and more equitable school system. Instead of just complaining and playing the victim, he needed to become part of the solution by working for change within the system, first, by welcoming all students into his classes, and second, by treating them fairly and equitably in his classroom.

This year, in my rounds of Eastern USA High, I still stop by Marco's brightly decorated classroom. As he meticulously corrects his student assignments and checks notebooks, I listen to his litany, complaining of unfair, poorly prepared students, and so on. I remind him to be proactive, call parents, hold on to consistent routines, prepare for the class, and be humble. I smile as I walk out the door. I know that the students are in good hands. We both feel pride when he informs me that former students have returned to tell him that they have appreciated his stern resolve to hold them to a higher standard. These words of encouragement keep Marco planning and correcting, even until 7 PM on a Friday night. They reinforce in me the idea that friendships can be forged through the pain and hard work of reflective mentoring.

Reflective Questions

- How does the "savior mentality" inhibit a healthy mentoring experience?

- What happens when the boundary between mentor and friendship becomes blurred? How can a mentoring relationship be salvaged once the lines have been crossed?

- How can a mentor be effective and resilient if he or she feels or is accused of being in collusion with a broken education system?

- If a friendship does develop between a mentor and mentee, how can you balance the two relationships so that the mentor is not mentoring twenty-four hours a day?

- If one of the goals of mentoring is teacher empowerment, how can we help teachers to stay focused on student learning and achievement and their own professional development along a continuum rather than focus on the external and sometimes negative forces that derail education?

CONCLUSION

What Can We Learn?

*A*s a team, we read and reread the transcripts of four years' worth of mentor interviews and we agreed that development and growth of the mentors seems to be linked to the way they negotiate this new professional role. To do this, mentors figure out how to facilitate, negotiate, and ameliorate relationships with their mentees and the other people in the schools within which they work, and they learn ways to approach and facilitate pedagogical skills in all kinds of mentees.

Describing the real lives of mentors as they work with mentees has been an incredible journey. We have come to understand the enormous complexities of the work and have tried to document how and in what ways mentors learn their role. It is another kind of teaching role, one that must be forged within the tensions that occur because mentors deal not only with their mentees but also with the culture of each school.

Having been chosen because of their excellence in teaching, mentors quickly find themselves searching for who they are, what their work really is, and how to feel confident in their new identity. To gain this confidence, mentors must learn the dynamics of different school cultures, deal with principals with varying leadership styles and expectations, find a way to gain respect in their new role, and develop a way of working as they are negotiating these new complexities. What we see is that mentors, similar to their mentees, do plenty of learning on the job as well as participating in continual professional development. In the process of figuring out what they are doing in these different contexts, they gain confidence and eventually become full-fledged mentors—respected for their expertise in their new professional role.

Part of the mentor's learning is to build trusting relationships, not only with the mentee but also with the adult community in the school. Principals, resource teachers, veteran teachers, and other administrators are all a part of creating the culture of the school. Somehow the mentor must find a way to figure out how to be brokers, facilitators, teachers, and protectors in order to be successful mentors. These roles change depending on the context of the school and the relationships with their mentees and the other adults in the school.

We learn that there are contexts that are extremely challenging for mentors, for example, going into a dysfunctional school or having experienced only an elementary school and finding themselves in a high school. Sometimes veteran teachers have a particular hold on what is acceptable in a school; lack of resources presents other problems for the new teacher; mandates and scripts make it hard for mentors to teach the fundamentals to novice teachers; and when a school is depressing or dysfunctional it is doubly hard for the mentor (and mentee) to feel good about their future in the teaching profession. But these contexts are part of what mentors learn to negotiate as part of their education in this new role.

Perhaps the heart of the tensions that mentors face is how to accelerate growth in the mentee, regardless of the culture of the school. Mentors learn that the ultimate tension for them is how to connect to their mentees in a mutually trusting relationship, one that enables mentors to continue to learn and improve their pedagogical skills, strategies, and abilities. But saying it is easier than doing it. Mentees differ. Some are open and others are defensive and reticent. Some are naturally friendly and others are protective and sometimes shy. Some can quickly label their needs and others seem overwhelmed with their teaching tasks. All of them need different approaches to building a relationship or advancing their teaching. And only with experience can the mentor learn how to approach mentees differently. Making friends is fine, but it must eventually lead to learning to teach better. The negotiations demand flexibility, sensitivity, reflection, support, and a heavy dose of thoughtful intelligence!

Few if any of the mentors would call themselves leaders, yet working through the tensions of mentoring, leadership skills, attitudes, and behaviors is exactly what the mentors are learning. Leadership in a number of ways is learned by negotiating the tensions within which mentors find themselves. Some learn the skills of change agentry when they are in situations where a wrong must be righted or in difficult situations that need to be brokered. Mentors learn that working in a new school culture (which is larger than their own classroom) demands that they think and work more systemically. Their world grows much larger than planning for their students. Different parts of the culture can impinge on their work with mentees. When possible, mentors should organize groups who learn to collaborate with one another. And sometimes mentors find themselves in situations where they must vocally advocate and fight against injustices because they are often in positions where they see the larger picture in a school.

Because mentors represent principles of good practice, they need to learn how to negotiate their way through the social system of the school. These are important aspects of the growing leadership responsibilities that mentors need to learn. The struggle to negotiate difficult situations, which turn out to be ubiquitous in many schools, is just the kind of experience that teaches mentors the complexity of their work and helps them develop a leadership stance. Nothing shows this better than the vignettes included in this book.

Seeing the mentors describe their work in the context of the schools where they work gives us a real sense of the complexity and difficulties of mentoring work. We learn how mentors work when new teachers are isolated in their schools from other adults and witness the toll it takes on the new teacher. In Story One, we come to understand how, when mentors are sensitive to the problems that a career changer might have, consistency with pedagogical help and empathy provides the mentee with new learnings, despite a dysfunctional system.

In Story Two, we learn how a mentor works to see beyond the negative attributes of the system. In this case, although Mr. Z gets a negative evaluation and is eventually fired, the mentor believes strongly that the mentee has creativity and real strengths as a novice teacher, despite this evaluation. The mentor persists in eventually finding this mentee a position in an alternative school where he blossoms with the greater flexibility of the school and becomes a well-respected and successful teacher.

In Story Three, we see a fairly typical situation in which the mentee claims to have no problems and the mentor has to find a way to build trust in the relationship and move the pedagogy forward. In addition, the mentor feels uncomfortable because her mentee is a high school teacher and her experience has been only in elementary schools. It is here we learn how creative mentors learn as they struggle with their own demons (feeling insecure) as well as those of the mentees (feeling defensive about their teaching). Not being afraid to expose these concerns allows mentor and mentee to understand that focusing on students helps the defensiveness of the mentee and then helps the mentor negotiate a legitimate way to help the novice teacher despite her initial insecurities.

Story Four teaches us about the integral growth of the mentor and the mentee. The beginning teacher blames the students for his lack of success with them. The mentor sets to work first trying to save the mentee by "telling" him what to do. When that doesn't work he tries to befriend him and make him feel more at ease. But that also has limited success. Finally, the mentor decides to enroll with his mentee in a Critical Friends Group Training where the objective is to learn to ask good questions and to become more reflective about one's practice. Little by little the mentor learns to deflect the criticisms that the mentee states with constancy, and the mentee learns painstakingly that he can improve his teaching by engaging student participation and learning.

These stories of mentoring in context teach us how mentors learn to constantly and consistently negotiate the pressures and problems of complicated and difficult school cultures and how the tensions of mentoring provide the grist for learning to lead. The mentors learned powerful lessons about their work and their progress by writing their stories, and it became evident that learning for mentors was synonymous with the struggle to wade through difficult situations and figure out how to manage them. Putting their stories down on paper helped the mentors get a hold of their knowledge in a way that showed them their progress over time and provides us with the real-life learning of these mentors and their growth as leaders.

Mentor Prompts

*H*ere's a helpful exercise that we use in our workshops. It's great for use on your own or in a group setting. Select one of the five tensions that you feel resonates most strongly with you at this time (you may want to refer to the handy snapshot of the five tensions later in this Appendix). After selecting the tension, reflect on your experience to date with that tension in mind. Using the prompts, if they're useful to you, write an example of a challenge that you've faced that describes what the tension feels like in practice.

- Write a short description of the tension.

- How did the tension arise?

- What did you do?

- What action did you take?

- What did you learn about your role as a mentor?

A Snapshot of the Five Mentor Tensions

TENSION ONE: Building a New Identity

- Mentors learn to adjust to their new role.

- Mentors deal with differing expectations of the "expert" role.

- Mentors learn how to work in a new culture.

TENSION TWO: Developing Trusting Relationships

- Mentors learn how to conduct intricate negotiations with veteran teachers and the principal.

- Mentors figure out how to work as an outsider who needs to develop trusting relationships.

TENSION THREE: Accelerating Teacher Development

- Mentors provide emotional support while focusing on instructional content in relationships with their mentees that are complex and challenging.

- Mentors learn the ways to help teachers develop and improve their practice.

TENSION FOUR: Mentoring in Challenging Contexts

- Mentors work in contexts where they have had little experience and knowledge.

- Mentors deal with tensions resulting from working in low-performing schools or schools that have mandates such as the use of scripted curricula.

TENSION FIVE: Learning Leadership Skills

- Mentors use leadership skills such as brokering resources for new teachers, creating and supporting effective communities of practice, and being an advocate for social justice while understanding and negotiating what mentors can and cannot influence.
- Mentors balance doing the job and being directed.

The Continual Professional Growth of Teacher Mentors

	Year One	Year Two	Year Three
Identity	• Adjusts from classroom teacher to teacher of teachers • Sees oneself as a beginning teacher coach	• Expands understanding of coaching role • Obtains a broader perspective of schools	• Becomes proficient and confident in teacher mentor role across schools • Feels valued as a professional teacher mentor • Sees self as a part of a larger profession
Role	• Enters a new school or schools • Establishes new relationships • Learns to work as an outsider while building trusting relationships • Becomes aware of complexity of mentor role	• Becomes familiar with staff and school culture at existing school • Becomes aware of complexity of mentor role in a deeper way • Has more clarity about his or her stance with administrators and confidentiality issues • May use entry skills at a newly assigned school(s)	• Becomes proficient at entering new schools and establishing new relationships • Expands understanding of varying school cultures • Establishes trust with several administrators and veteran teachers

	Year One	Year Two	Year Three
Supporting Beginning Teachers	• Receives extensive training in how to coach and use instructional coaching tools • Observes many teachers teach • Tries to respond to a variety of beginning teacher needs	• Gains more experience coaching a variety of teachers across different contexts • Feels competent using different assessment tools • Continues to learn in mentor learning community • Becomes more adept at moving from emotional to instructional coaching	• Becomes a confident teacher coach with experience supporting a variety of teachers across different contexts • Knows how to navigate support for teachers with different needs • Knows how to apply targeted focus on improving instruction • Continues to value mentor learning community to solve challenges
Leadership Skills	• Provides new leadership experiences • Facilitates new teacher learning individually and in small groups	• Sees opportunities to support improved instruction across classrooms • May take more initiative to support learning teams • May help district plan for beginning teacher support	• May be asked to take a formal role facilitating grade level or department professional learning communities • Works with administrators on strategic issues at school • Facilitates mentor learning community

	Year One	Year Two	Year Three
Advocate for School Improvement	• Focuses on learning skills to improve teaching of assigned mentees • Obtains broader perspective of teacher working conditions	• Sees potential power of role • Has greater insight as to what one can (and cannot) influence as a mentor	• Has expanded understanding of school systems • Advocates for good working conditions and fair evaluation practices of beginning teachers • Willing to take risks on behalf of teachers
Career Planning	• Adjusts to new job • Focuses on learning to be an excellent teacher coach and a new career opportunity	• Assesses satisfaction being a teacher coach and career goals • May miss working directly with students • May adore coaching and facilitating adult group learning	• May want to continue in role of teacher mentor • May have expanded career goals • May enroll in administrative credential program • May plan to return to classroom teaching • May desire a hybrid job of mentoring and teaching students

INDEX

building a new identity, 2,
11–19; developing
trusting relationships,
2–3, 23–34, 142; learning
leadership skills, 5,
53–62, 143–144; lessons
learned about
overcoming, 141–146;
mentoring in challenging
contexts, 4, 45–50,
142–143

Mentor-mentee stories:
"Finding a Way" on
mentoring Angela, 107,
109–119, 145; "Fired,
Hired, and Inspired" on
mentoring Mr. Z, 83,
85–104, 145; lessons
learned from, 145–146;
"Savior, Friend, Mentor"
on mentoring Marco,
123, 125–139, 146; "The
Waiting Place" on
mentoring Mr. N, 67,
69–80, 145

Mentoring in challenging
contexts: confusion over
unspoken rules, 47–48;
difficult school culture,
47–48; economically
marginalized school
population, 49–50;
ineffective veteran
teachers, 46; learning to
navigate an unfamiliar
school culture, 49–50;

lessons learned on,
142–143; mentoring
without subject-matter
expertise, 48–49; overly
focused on test scores,
46–47; overview of, 4;
personal development of
mentors in facing, 50;
struggling with reduced
budgets, 50; traumatic
situations, 117–118, 119

Mr. N (mentee): facing
behavior challenges with
kindness, 73–74; on his
first year experience,
72–73; initial visit with,
70–71; introduction to,
69–70; laid off due to
budget cuts, 78; lessons
learned from story of,
145; logistical test pro-
blems faced by students
of, 76–77; moving on
from "waiting place" to
face the future, 78–79;
reflective questions on
mentee experience of, 80;
student academic chal-
lenges faced by, 76–77;
teaching classroom
management to, 74–76.
See also Baldacci, Leslie
(mentor teacher)

Mr. Z (mentee): alternative
school placement of,
101–102; career change

162